Bob Orrell, RE
27th July 1918 – 30th June 2004

The
Regimental Piano

Major Bob Orrell, RE

A Story of War, Love & Peace... From a Bunker on
D-Day to a Peace Village in Vietnam

To

THE REGIMENTAL PIANO

Major Bob Orrell, RE

by Tim Parker

With my best ...

HOP Publishing

THE REGIMENTAL PIANO
Major Bob Orrell; RE.

The Regimental Piano is about the life of Major Bob Orrell, Royal Engineers.
The story starts in the Great Depression following the First World War and follows one man's call of duty to help rid Europe of the Nazis in the Second World War, a journey which took him through the trials and tribulations of life, through D-Day and, via the Bailey bridge, finding love.

Bob's later life was as a fervent campaigner for world peace.

This book is the joint copyright of:

Tim Parker
and
HOP Publishing
HOP House
41 Church Road
Hove
BN3 2BE

Printed in Great Britain by:

Reprint LLC Limited
47 Highcroft Villas
Brighton
BN1 5PT.

First Edition – 18th December 2013 to commemorate the forthcoming 70th Anniversary of D-Day.

Tim Parker
Copyright © HOP Publishing

FOREWORD

Bob Orrell of the Royal Engineers distinguished himself in the Second World War, in particular in the D-Day landings on Sword Beach, Normandy, in 1944, for which he was mentioned in Dispatches.

In Ouistreham, there is still a concrete bunker standing 60ft high, with walls some 10ft thick, overlooking Sword Beach. Once the control tower for German guns placed there to foil an Allied invasion, today it houses a museum commemorating the Allied landing. Lieutenant Orrell, as he was then, managed to capture the bunker and its 53 inmates with the aid of a crane, two men and a lot of courage.

Bob Orrell's family was in the cotton trade, mill owners who took an Owenite approach to the care of their workers. Compassion and a sense of fairness were traits which Bob shared and exhibited throughout his life. He had no doubt that Hitler's Nazis had to be defeated, and he joined the Army in 1940, conducting himself with courage and integrity. Once the war was over, however, he rejected militarism.

In 1980, his wife, Nancy, took him to see the film The War Game. Overnight he joined CND and was soon chairman of its Christchurch and New Forest branch. He soon became Chairman of Ex-Services CND and worked tirelessly, even travelling to Russia. Nancy was herself active at Greenham Common, where she was arrested and sent to Holloway prison. She would not let Bob pay her fine.

A year or two after he joined CND, Bob Orrell attended his first D-Day reunion at Ouistreham, handing out CND leaflets to his old comrades. He told his friends and family: 'It was the bravest thing I ever did.'

Tony Benn, September 2013

["Owenite": After the 19th Century social philosopher Robert Owen who advocated the reform of society according to communitarian and cooperative principles]

By the same author

- Signalman Jones
- The Last Voyage of the Shelduck

For
NANCY
And in memory of
ROBERT

With special thanks to:

Nancy Orrell
Christine Orrell
Martin Orrells (both!)
Fabrice & Brigitte Corbin
Nicolas Dumont

For their contributions and

Tim Parker: Again, author – he is great!
Keith Pengilly: Advice and printing;
Drew Dickson: Editing in Stockport;
Cenk Nuttall: Graphics in Hove;
John Honeysett: Research;
Liz Bulman: Typing & admin

Photographs
Bournemouth Evening Echo
Jo Renshaw and Hilary Webb

Illustrations
Bailey & Uniflote Handbook
The world famous Conrad J Lowen – war artist
Thanks to Royal Engineers for permission to print "The work of the Royal Engineers on D-Day" sketches

Front Cover Artwork
Bente Bjornbakk in Norway and Big Art Canvas of Brighton

December 2013

Contents

Photographs and Illustrations

Bob as a soldier and veteran by Conrad Lowen

1

Early Years

On the morning of June 5, 1944, 'Ike' – General Eisenhower, the Supreme Commander of the Allied Forces in Europe – was walking along the Southsea Promenade, Portsmouth, as I led my troop of Royal Engineers down a rickety pier head to board our landing craft. We had been told to split our force into different craft to improve the chances that a reasonable number of us would survive. Nobody was under any illusion; it would be a hard job and God knows what risk we would face to life and limb when our turn came to land on Sword Beach in Normandy. 'That must be Ike,' someone said as we boarded our craft.

Prior to that fateful day, we had spent a month under canvass in the Sussex countryside, camped near Billingshurst, waiting for orders to move on to Portsmouth. The weather had been poor and while some leave had been granted, security was very tight and there was little for us to do. I had spent a good deal of the time thinking about my family. I was sorry that my mother had died so young, she would have been so pleased that I was now a lieutenant with the Royal Engineers. And then there were my friends in Tottington. Would I see the place again? And what about my father, now a tobacconist in Bury, when previously he had managed the town mill. What a let-down. But I have to confess that most of my thoughts had centred on Nancy, a marvellous dark-haired girl from Christchurch who was now a nurse. Nancy was special.

There had been much talk in the camp about the coming conflict and, of course, we all knew about the utter disaster of the Dieppe landing some two years previously when many good men had lost their lives. Nevertheless, morale was high and while none of us took any pleasure in the prospect of risking our lives in an invasion of France, there was a steely resolve in all of us to ensure that Hitler and his Nazi Party were destroyed.

I was born in July 1918 in Tottington, a Lancashire town now part of Greater Manchester, when Britain was at war with Germany. But the end was not too far away and an Armistice signed on 11 November brought the fighting to a halt. Of course, I was far too young to know anything about the war but my parents, Fred and Annie Orrell, could never have thought that just 22 years later their son would be on his way to France to fight the Germans again in the Second World War, a conflict which proved even worse than the war which had just ended.

I can remember very little of my early days in Tottington but in the time between the wars the town was a good place to live. It was run by an urban district council, which was well managed by its councillors, and had an excellent school with good facilities. The Church of St Anne held the community together and Tottington had its own cotton mill, Walshaw Mill, which helped bring employment, housing and prosperity to the town. I cannot pretend that it was much of a place to look at – it was a very small town with just one main street, Booth Street. But for me its great attraction was that it was near to the open countryside which I loved.

My father, Fred, was born an Orrell. Orrell, I later learned, was one of the most important and respected names in all of Lancashire. Fred married Annie, my mother, a member of the Warburton Family, who had many business interests, pubs, property and farms. The Warburtons were always very busy – too busy, some said. There was sometimes an undercurrent of disapproval about their dealings.

As I have grown older, I have begun to sense that I owe it to my family and friends to write something about my memories of Tottington and, indeed, my life. I have always been something of a hoarder and, as a result, have gathered a remarkable collection of photographs, documents and memorabilia, which I hope will give everyone, and in particular my family, interest and pleasure. I, too, am a winner, as this task has brought back many good memories of my family, who make me very proud. So, Christine, Robert, Jonathan, Martin and Nancy, together with your families, this is dedicated to you.

Memories of my very early youth are vague and scanty but I do remember getting chickenpox at the same time as electricity was being installed in our house, at 174 Booth Street. To make things worse, while the work was being done I stepped on a nail in an upturned floorboard. It was very, very painful – something I have never forgotten. And I remember Booth Street well enough. It contained an almost continuous line of bright, well-built red-brick terraced houses, each with a small paved back yard housing a WC and a coal shed. All the houses in the street were very much the same.

As an only child, I was rather spoilt but I was happy and tried to do what was required of me. For some reason, in spite of having a friendly and sometimes boisterous nature, I tended to shun group activities, such as the Scouts, Sunday school and organised games. I valued my independence and was at my happiest walking and cycling on my own.

Later, I got on well at Tottington Primary School. The headmaster once asked me what I wanted to do when I grew up.

'Be an inventor,' I told him.

'And where do you think you would get your money from?'

I never really got over that but for many years clung to my ideal, which was to produce something original and useful to mankind from my own head. Still, my primary school taught me a lot and helped me win a scholarship to Bury Grammar School. It was at a time when Manchester's great cotton industry was in trouble and a good education became even more important.

I would like to tell you a bit more about my parents: my mother was not well for much of her life and sometimes my father was a little overbearing and rather bossy. So in family disputes I always sided with my mother, and did my best to help her with her housework. Sadly, my mother died when she was 49 and I was 21. Only then, too late of course, did I realise how much I had loved her.

I would not like you to think that my father was in any way a bad man; he was not. In fact, he was a good man with many qualities – a great sense of humour and a strong and dynamic personality – who was, in many ways, ahead of his time. He worked his way through all the cotton-weaving jobs at Walshaw Mill and went to night school. He had a sympathetic understanding of peoples' needs, and when he became manager of the mill he set up a works canteen so that the workers got a decent meal. He also started a scheme to give women more time off for childbirth (at that time women were required to be back at their looms the day after they had given birth).

But, early in the 1930s the mill was shut down because there was no longer enough work to keep it open. My father and a few others stayed on to prevent it becoming derelict. Despite my father weaving some cloth and touring Lancashire in an effort to find new business, the mill never reopened. But my dad was a fighter and, in an attempt to restore the family fortunes, he bought a wholesale and retail tobacconist in nearby Bury town centre.

Tottington, as you will have gathered, was a tight-knit community and most of my two families – the Orrells and the Warburtons – lived in the vicinity. My grandfather, Robert Grindwood Orrell, was a fine figure of a man and a pillar of society, who in his time was a Church Warden and general manager of Walshaw Mill. Once a week he would make a visit to the great city of Manchester, then the world centre of the cotton manufacturing industry. In the early days after the First World War most of the surrounding towns depended on the cotton mills for their livelihoods, so the collapse of the industry was a disaster, which added to the country's terrible Depression and mass unemployment. I never knew my grandfather as a person – he was perhaps a bit too grand – but I liked his wife, Alice. She always gave me a half crown on New Year's Day and a drop of whisky in my tea so I could be like the grown-ups.

Another character who I can just remember is my great grandmother, Ellen Warburton, who married a legendary character known as 'Red Jim', a raffish fellow, larger than life and full of mischief. They lived in a small stone-built house at the end of a row of six cottages and some farm buildings. The house was set on a ridge, the highest point in Tottington district, running north to south, which had once carried the old Roman road Watling Street. Their house was in a desolate location but it gave me my first introduction to the magic of the wide open spaces. To the west and south sprawled the cotton manufacturing towns of Bolton and Bury, punctured by tall mill chimneys making their contribution to the pall of smoke, which could obscure much of the area from view. As a young man, I spent many hours on those hillsides as an articled pupil to the local surveyor and sanitary inspector, timing the emission of smoke from the various chimneys. One of my earliest tasks in this, my first job, was to escort the Tottington midwife to the adjoining hamlet of Affetside when it was completely snowbound. On a later occasion, I organised a cutting through snow two yards deep to relieve the village.

To the north and east the landscape was framed by the hills and moors of the Pennine Range, dominated by the rounded peaks of Holcombe Hill, which was topped by a monument to Sir Robert Peel, the founder of the police force. Then there was Knowle Hill, my 'private chapel'. I spent very many happy days walking over those lonely hills with their cotton grass and bogs and where the landscape was full of surprises. Unexpected valleys would suddenly appear, revealing hidden reservoirs together with the remains of earlier cotton mills and hamlets built for water and power processing. There were early water wheels and old steam engines, which used poor coal dug from the nearby hillsides to drive them.

In medieval times Tottington was nothing more than an agricultural settlement but the area was well known for its good hunting and had some grand dwellings. Consequently, it became known as a 'Fee', the equivalent of a Royal Manor. In 1155, the Orrell family (which had its own coat of arms), led by Sir Richard De Orrell, owned much land and wielded great power throughout Lancashire. Our family's ancestry can be traced from Sir Richard to the present day, so the places that I roamed as a young man would have been known to Sir Richard and our Orrell ancestors, who would have hunted for deer and wild boar on those marvellous hills and open land, a thought that has always given me great pleasure.

Looking back now, I wish I had learned more about Ellen and Red Jim. They had 13 children together, 11 of whom survived to adulthood. How they got on so well on that isolated hill with all those children I will never know.

Then there was my mother's youngest sister, Aunt Rachel, who always took a very close interest in my welfare. Indeed, after my mother died, she gave up her house in Bolton, where she was senior mistress at the grammar school. She was a great support and an active organiser. Bright and clever, she had done very well at university and taught at a number of schools, where she was loved and respected. I still miss her, but it was a comfort that our family nursed her in our home before she died. I must mention Rachel's great friend, Joyce Martin, who became a major during the Second World War and adopted our family as her own.

When I was 11 and the time came for me to leave my junior school, I was apprehensive. From being near the top of a small school to being a junior at a big school is nerve-wracking and there was no bigger or more important school in our part of Lancashire than Bury Grammar. A traditional and respected institution set in the town centre, the school was divided by a road – on one side the girls' school and on the other the boys'. In those days few pupils, boy or girl, would have had the nerve to lift their eyes to see what was happening on the other side.

I enjoyed my time at Bury Grammar and found the work interesting and rewarding. It was an easy journey from Tottington to Bury, just two-and-a-half miles, so I could cycle or walk as the mood took me. Of course, all the while I was growing up to become quite a strong young man. I even did a bit of boxing, which would help me later. I was lucky that, as I grew up, I had plenty of friends but at heart I guess I was still something of a loner with my own views on life and how things should be done.

I left the grammar school when I was 17. I didn't go to university but became an articled pupil to a Mr Laurence Kenyon, the Surveyor and Sanitary Inspector for Tottington Urban District Council. My boss gave me a remarkably free hand, and to become qualified I worked largely on my own and through correspondence courses. But it was becoming increasingly apparent that another war with Germany was inevitable, that Hitler and his Nazi Party would accept no compromise, that appeasement was tosh and that my life and the lives of millions of others were about to change. Strangely enough, the country re-arming for another war with Germany benefited millions of workers to begin with. The Depression came to an end. Anything in those days was better than being out of work when state benefits were, for all practical purposes, almost non-existent. But most people in the country were patriotic – 'We will give the Huns a bloody good hiding' was a popular refrain. I have a clear memory of Prime Minister Chamberlain's broadcast, which I heard on our crystal radio set in September 1939 when war was finally declared: 'This morning the British Ambassador in Berlin handed the German Government a final note stating that unless we heard from them by 11am that they were prepared at once to withdraw their troops from Poland, a state of war would exist between usI have to tell you that no such undertaking has been received and that, consequently, this country is at war with Germany.'

I was given a degree of deferment so that I could finish my exams. On that score all went well and in 1940 I received the good news that I had been awarded the gold medal from the Institution of Municipal and County Engineers for my Testamur Examination. I was on my way as a civil engineer.

2

I Join The Army And Find Nancy

I had become convinced that Hitler and his Nazi Party had to be defeated, so I first threw all my energy into making sure that Tottington was well defended. Being far from the centre of the war zone made no difference as far as I was concerned, and I have to say that I was given much help and assistance from the local community, except perhaps from the Quakers.

So it turned out that during my last year in Tottington while still employed by the council, I spent most of my time devoted to air-raid precaution work. I was in charge of rescue, the control centre and much else. Our town clerk was a Quaker and my boss was fairly old, so in reality the medical officer and I ran the whole show, including all the Civil Defence services. We made arrangements for message-taking, we trained men for rescue work and dealing with gas attacks as well as training auxiliary fire fighters, wardens and civil defence personnel. We strengthened buildings, shoring them up against air raids, built shelters and even went so far as to dig trenches, which must have puzzled enemy aircraft flying overhead. I have to say that I enjoyed myself and learned very quickly how I could lead. It was fun teaching our rescue men how they might move heavy objects safely, lifting large lumps of metal, such as an old Lancashire Boiler weighing 20 tons, with the help of levers and rollers – there was little mechanical equipment around in those days.

As it happened, it was not until Christmas 1944 that Tottington was attacked by the enemy, when it was hit by a V1 flying bomb released by plane over the Pennines. The damage was severe and part of Tottington's town centre was devastated.

In July 1940, when I had finished my exams, I joined the Army. To my surprise I found myself volunteered for the Royal Army Medical Corp, probably because the authorities had seen that I had previously worked for a sanitary inspector. It took a bit of sorting out but finally I was transferred to the Royal Engineers, where my first job was in the cookhouse. Still, after my basic training I was recommended for officer training at the Royal Engineers School in Aldershot. There, to my surprise, I had the distinction of coming first in my class and was promoted to a second lieutenant.

I was then posted to the 9th Armoured Division of the 11th Field Squadron. The 11th Field Squadron was a new division, which was getting ready for engagement overseas and was reckoned to be the crack unit at the time. I enjoyed my time with the 9th and was much impressed when General Montgomery came to talk to us. Somehow or other he made us believe that we would win the war. We cheered him to the echo and all felt better.

In December 1941, while still serving with the 9th, I had a bad fall. I was involved in an interdivisional despatch riding competition and took a tumble over the handlebars. The accident turned out to be a disaster. Despite wearing a crash helmet, I lost my sense of balance and could not walk a straight line but, much worse, I was unable to speak properly. The doctors told me there was something wrong with my cerebellum and I spent several months in a military hospital. But slowly I forced myself to get better and, wanting to get back in the Army, I went for an interview in London, where I persuaded the authorities that, with my engineering background, I could still be useful. A few days later, in August 1942, I was posted to Christchurch at the newly formed Experimental Bridging Establishment and became an experimental officer in bridge building. The centre was led by the world famous Sir Donald Bailey. It was the best move I could have made.

When I arrived in Christchurch I was still downgraded medically but was given an interesting job in the test house, testing materials and parts of bridges to destruction. Later, with the military, I helped put together Bailey bridges of all shapes and sizes before once again testing them. It was in Christchurch that I met the girl who was to become my wife – a lovely dark-haired girl called Nancy.

I found the work at the bridging unit intensely interesting, particularly as, never having been to university, I had had little practical experience of how materials behaved under pressure. It was also a marvellous opportunity for me to learn from the Experimental Bridging Establishment's top-class engineers who, without exception, treated me very kindly.

Whilst at Christchurch, we organised occasional concerts for the men and staff. These were often fun affairs, but we got proper song sheets printed. It was something we all looked forward to; it was a good antidote to our labours and perhaps kept our mind off the war from time to time.

I enjoyed myself in Christchurch and slowly but surely felt my health coming back to me. There were a number of very interesting personalities in the unit and Sir Donald Bailey himself, besides being a remarkable engineer and inventor, was an extraordinarily nice man. I was very fortunate. One of my particular friends, with whom I worked closely, was Ron Taylor, a very good Structural Engineer who was subsequently drafted for special training overseas and for a time worked behind enemy lines in Italy. It was Ron who introduced me to Nancy, who worked near Sir Donald Bailey's office.

Ron knew Nancy's family. Things had been difficult for her at home. Her father had died very young, leaving her, her brother Ted, her mother and her energetic younger sister with little money. Somehow the small family got by sewing dresses and coats but were so often short of food and warmth. Nancy was bright and won a scholarship to Brockenhurst School. When she was 15, Ron had rescued her from a dead-end job at the bank and found her a position in Sir Donald's office. 'Mr Bailey is a marvellous man,' Nancy told me later. 'When I deliver his mail, he always stops what he is doing and talks to me.' In one way I suppose the war worked out well for Nancy and for her brother, Ted, who become a pilot and loved the Royal Air Force, flew Dakotas. At the end of the war Ted was stationed in the Far East and plans were being made to get all the servicemen home. By then, there was a lot of faith in the trusty Dakotas and the Commanding Officer told the men that any crew members who knew the pilot was good enough could start planning to fly back to England. All Ted's crew persuaded him to fly back and they each bought a local carpet to take home. Very severe stormy weather over the English Channel meant that Ted had them all ready to jettison the lot, but Ted, a great pilot, got everyone and their belongings safely back to England.

There were many characters working at our establishment. One of the best known was Doctor Otto Bondi, a famous structural engineer who had swum the Rhine to get out of Austria when the Germans invaded. He was an extremely clever engineer who knew all about welding. He also developed the use of the Bailey bridge as a suspension bridge with a view to crossing the Rhine. He knew what he was doing and was good fun. And, of course, never far away was Nancy. I had fallen for her in a big way – did she know?

I have sometimes been asked why Bailey bridges were so important to our armies during the last war. The answer is that Donald Bailey's work made it possible for trained men to build great bridges capable of carrying heavy loads within a matter of hours, thus enabling our soldiers, together with their tanks, equipment and heavy armour to cross major obstacles very quickly, something that was crucial in modern warfare. All the Bailey bridge equipment was designed to be transportable by a six-man team and could, when assembled, carry the heaviest of our tanks.

Although I had been very happy at Christchurch, after a year I found that, more than anything, I wanted to move on. I was not an official member of staff and to some extent I was a 'spare hand' there. Moreover, I had become a little careless, once, unusually for me, breaking a bridge by running tanks over it too quickly. Not long after that incident, and having been passed 'Grade A' Fit, I joined a new unit, the 91st Field Company. Of course, I was sad to leave Nancy but I would see her again, I was sure of it. And so it was that in October1943 I left the Experimental Bridging Establishment. Just a week or two later Nancy left, too, to take up a position as a nurse in Boscombe Hospital.

I soon found that the new unit I had joined was in serious training for the second front and it became clear that we were going to be a specialist beach unit engaged in heavy bridging. The job of a Royal Engineers beach unit was to clear and look after the area where troops landed, then see that all the roads were in good order, enabling the troops to get forward the moment they left their landing craft. My job was to be a reconnaissance officer, probing ahead, looking for problems and searching for solutions. I enjoyed the job, even though I had to put my trust in another motorcycle.

We first trained in Northamptonshire, then moved on to Ross and Cromarty in Northern Scotland, bridging the Black Isle. I did an underwater-assaults-and-demolition course, which taught me how to blow up obstacles on the beach, mainly steel girders. It was strenuous and a little scary but I had no health problems now. As we headed back down south, security became very tight. We were all under strict instructions and were not allowed any contact with the civilian population. Finally, we made camp near Billingshurst in West Sussex, which brings me back to D-Day.

3

We Sail For France

Finally on board our landing craft, we sailed into the Solent. Years later I read that the rumour was true, it was indeed General Eisenhower who had walked along the Southsea Promenade on June 5 and had seen us embark. Ike had already postponed D-Day because of the weather and, I suspect, he would have taken an anxious look to seaward, hoping as much as we did that the landings would take place the following day.

The Solent itself was the most amazing and spectacular sight I had ever seen: ships and craft of every type as far as the eye could see, and in the dim distance some queer objects which looked like a floating town. These, we were soon to discover, were part of the prefabricated components of the Mulberry harbour used by the Allies to unload cargo on to the beaches. Later, I learned that Nancy, too, had witnessed the invasion fleet from a headland near Christchurch and there, too, the sea, from the Needles on her left to Swanage on her right, was alive with ships. For her it was an unforgettable sighting of the greatest armada the world had ever seen.

Our company, like all the others, was split among many landing craft, all phased to arrive on the beaches at different times. There were a few officers on board who crowded together in a tiny wardroom while the rest of our craft was packed with troops.

As we sailed that night for France we knew that the invasion was finally on. At daybreak we found we were sailing in convoy with a long line of ships well out into the English Channel, an exciting and inspiring sight. At last the coast of France appeared in the distance and we could make out warships, tank landing craft, battleships, destroyers and other ships of every conceivable size and shape. The warships were firing regular salvos and rocket ships spewed their awe-inspiring, flaming missiles from time to time, which screeched their way to the shore. There was some slight opposition from one of the buildings on the seafront but that was soon silenced. However, the land and coast to the east of Ouistreham remained in enemy hands and shelling from that direction was a problem for some weeks.

Above, the sky was as crowded as the sea: squadrons of transport planes towing gliders passed overhead and a minute or two later a galaxy of gaily coloured parachutes descended just a mile or two inshore. Soon the transports returned, heading out to sea and for home, all except for one poor blighter shot down in flames from one of the houses on the seafront. Within a matter of minutes the house disintegrated. It seemed that every floating gun was intent on avenging those luckless airmen.

We must have been offshore, wallowing in the sea, for four hours before the signal came instructing our landing craft to beach. I was detailed to be the last person off the ship, so I went down to the hold to be with the chaps. Most of our men – in the throes of seasickness, their little paper bags at the ready – were looking shaky. It had been a smooth crossing but standing around in the hold of our craft with the powerful smell of diesel and an inshore swell was proving too much for most of us.

Eventually, the first detail was prepared to disembark. The troops went on deck but there was trouble with the ramps, which could not be let down on either side of the ship's bows. On the second attempt one of the ramps slipped off into the sea, taking three of our men with it. Only one of those men was saved, a grey-haired chap of about 50. Our medical officer attended to him. He was stripped of his clothes, given a blanket and told he would be sent back to England. Our ship's inability to beach was annoying, not to say dangerous, as the odd shell was fired at us from the shore. At last our skipper decided to ground the ship and most of us, including myself, got ashore without getting our feet wet.

It was about 1700 on June 6 when we picked our way up the litter-strewn Sword Beach, navigating our way through masses of wrecked vehicles, mainly our own, and other stuff bogged in the sand. We made towards the beach exit and then along a narrow path through the sand hills of La Breche to the roadway between Riva Bella and Lion-sur-Mer, which was to be our company's headquarters. On our way we passed the grey-haired man who had been tipped into the sea. He was still wrapped in the blanket that had been given to him by the ship's doctor. I have often wondered about him, who he was and whether he survived the war. As we threaded along through the sand hills I remember thinking to myself 'I am in France'. It was the first time I had ever been out of England.

On that first evening none of us really knew what was going on and we certainly had no sense of the tactical situation. There is a saying: 'the fog of war'. That certainly applied to us. Anyway, by nightfall we had got most of our field company together. I had assisted in rounding up stragglers by running up and down the beach on my lightweight motorbike, shepherding troops to the right exits. Later that evening we began to dig-in in a small, sandy field next to the road. There was firing a short distance inland and several houses on the seafront were burning, while others were still occupied by the enemy. I decided to have a look for some of our chaps and soon found Number 1 Platoon in an orchard. The men were all in good order, although one of their comrades had been lost, drowned on landing. There was little sign of life inland, so I returned to our unit to sleep in one of the holes we had dug. In the morning, water was something of a difficulty but I clearly remember we had beans for breakfast. There was also news about Nick, the other reconnaissance officer in our company. He had landed early with the commandoes charged with preventing the demolition of the lock gates at Riva Bella. He had done his job but got a bullet in his bottom and was on his way home to England. That might have been me, I thought to myself.

The D-Day landings comprised the largest and most complicated military operation that had ever been attempted. I am very proud of the part the 91st Field Company played in it. There were five invasion beaches – Utah, Omaha, Gold, Juno and Sword – with the landings stretching along the Normandy coast for over 40 miles. All the landings faced different problems and dangers but all were successful, despite some very heavy losses, particularly on the American beach, Omaha. The landing force on our beach, Sword, was under the command of General Sir Miles Dempsey and comprised mainly British troops. The most easterly of the landings, the task was to create a breach in the enemy defences wide enough to let through a wave of 29,000 troops, together with their weapons and equipment. Those troops had two objectives: to reinforce and relieve the British airborne troops near Benouville, and to capture Caen by nightfall; or at least that was the plan.

Landing the troops and getting their equipment ashore was brilliantly successful, as was the reinforcement of the British airborne troops, but capturing Caen took very much longer than expected. Consequently, our unit spent over a month in the Ouistreham area.

From D-Day plus one all of our men worked flat out. On that first morning we built two Bailey bridges, one across the Orne Canal and one across the river; both were competed by 0900. But our main concern was keeping the roads open and unloading ships, getting as much equipment ashore as quickly as possible. One of my main problems was the supply of water – it appeared that the yield from local wells had been affected by the Allied bombardment. Unfortunately, my talk with a French plumber was not a success – neither of us could understand the other. French lessons before we sailed for France would have been a real help, but I suspect it is too late for me to file a complaint now.

During that first afternoon there was a real blow to our plans when a single German Dornier bomber – the first we had seen – flew over and dropped just one bomb directly into our main beachhead stores. Petrol, ammunition and everything else was lost in less than half an hour.

In the evening of our first full day in France we moved our headquarters into some bungalows I had found in the residential part of Riva Bella, but we only there stayed there for one night after it transpired the whole area was infested with voracious mosquitoes. The next day we moved to higher ground about half a mile south of Ouistreham. That morning firing broke out and one shot missed our Sgt Major's head by inches. Rumour had it that Germans had been seen in the woods nearby. However, it turned out to be friendly fire – a troop of our Ack Ack boys had assumed that we were the enemy. I hopped on my motorbike and tore round to the troop, shouting: 'Please stop shooting at us, please!'

It may sound as though our men were moving around without much difficulty but this was not the case, we all had to move with great caution. Being engineers, we were always wary of mines, booby traps and other devices. Many were dummies but anti-personnel devices placed haphazardly by the roadside were extremely dangerous, as many found to their cost.

By the third night we had moved back into Ouistreham and were camping in an orchard, using some farm buildings as our company office and store. By then we were all so tired we could have slept anywhere

The next day, D-Day plus three, I continued my glorious wanderings. I went along to the foreshore at Riva Bella, east of where the landings had taken place. There was one large area of sand hills – it must have been a mile long – where the Germans had been building extensive concrete fortifications. One of our light anti-aircraft guns was now in position there. The whole area had apparently been built as a coastal battery, many underground bunkers were complete and at the side of the large gun positions were smaller pits with dummy guns. I prodded my way round, pricking the sand for mines with my bayonet. It was an eerie and lonely place and, to make matters worse, a number of our dead commandoes had been left lying in the sand (they were later buried by our company). But, to my delight, there was also a vast amount of building material and at least half a dozen concrete mixers, which could be extremely useful for our company. I also found a piano, which must have come from the German officers' mess.

Returning to our company HQ, I made a report on the materials I had found. I also described the strange tower I had seen but was unable to enter: 'It's a very solid looking concrete tower, some 60ft high, with no opening but a long slit at the top which looks as if it has received a direct hit. Its entrance is below ground and sealed by a solid steel door. From the number of cables leading into it, it appears that the building may be some sort of power house or control point.'

That afternoon (D-Day plus three) I returned with a three-ton lorry and our Motor Transport Sergeant, 'Big Jim', who was about the only man I could find in our camp. We intended to pick up as much as we could, including the piano, which I knew would have been good for morale in the days to come. Unfortunately, crossing a stretch of sand, our vehicle sank through the roof of a lightly covered trench and we had to spend most of the afternoon trying to dig it out. We were just 50 yards from the concrete tower. It was our crane that eventually did the job and we returned to our headquarters in the early evening. When we got back I found that, having read my report, our colonel wanted to know by the morning about the contents of the large tower. He wanted urgent intelligence about whether the site would be suitable for mixing concrete, which was needed for the roads from our beach head, and so I received orders to investigate the strange concrete tower.

So obeying orders, at about 2200 that night, Big Jim, myself, the crane driver and his mate returned to the strong point to investigate the contents of its forbidding tower. I took the mobile crane because at that time it was being used far less than any of our other transports.

It was dark by the time we got to the beach. We left the mobile crane on the road near to where we had been bogged down that afternoon. We had brought 14lb of explosive to use on the steel door. We first put about 7lb around its hinges. That should have been ample, but nothing was even dislodged. We then tried to lift the door off its hinges using ratchet jacks but again met with little success. The doors were a tougher proposition than we had anticipated. Working on the door of the bunker for some four hours by the light of our oil lamp, we began to worry about what we might find inside. There were times when we thought we heard noises and I had a strong feeling we were going to discover many dead or dying Germans. I did not relish the prospect. Finally, we placed the remainder of our explosive on both edges of the door, lit a fuse and retreated a reasonable distance as we could not be sure there were no further explosives inside the building. We later discovered there were a couple of cases of hand grenades just behind the entrance.

When we returned to the tower we found that we had managed to completely blow in the door. We tossed in a couple of hand grenades to put off anybody who might have been waiting for us inside and, when the smoke had cleared, went in to see what we could find. There was a great pile of equipment, including hand grenades, in a small room. Leading from that room was a well-stocked larder. There were steps leading upwards in one corner of the larder and as we turned our attention to them a voice suddenly called out in English 'Come upstairs, Johnny, it's all right!'

'Bugger that, you come down!' I shouted and the four of us scuttled out into the night. We placed our storm lantern at the entrance to the tower, drew back and waited. Eventually, two German officers came out. One spoke perfect English and explained that there were 53 men in the tower and they all wished to surrender.

I didn't trust the Jerry and fearing that when they saw how small we were in number they might well change their mind, I sent our crane driver's mate off to contact the gunners to try to get their support. We waited a long time for him to return and, finally losing patience, I told the German commander to send his men down one by one while our driver stood at the opening, giving them the once over as they came out. Jim looked after the two officers (we had relieved them of their pistols) and I formed all 53 of them into a long line under the muzzle of my Sten gun. Incidentally, I had never fired a Sten gun in my life – and Jim had only three rounds left in his.

Eventually, our driver's mate returned empty handed from his quest, so we marched our straggling party on to Riva Bella as we followed behind on our crane, occasionally flicking the spotlight on them before we turned them over to the military police compound without incident. But we kept hold of the young English-speaking officer and told him he would have to show us over the building, walking in front to spring any booby traps. It transpired that the mysterious tower was the control and headquarters building for the coastal battery. The Germans must have taken refuge there when they realised the size of the invasion force. Clearly, they had fired from its roof and were responsible for those of our commandoes who lay dead in the sand. I suppose they must have watched us with some amusement that afternoon as we tried to get our truck out of the ditch. Luckily for us, their wish not to disclose their position made them hold their fire.

The tower was crammed with materials, equipment and instruments of every kind. We took away three suitcases: one containing binoculars, one packed with pistols and one packed with various articles, which we distributed to our engineers back at camp. While we had been working away at the door of the tower, its inmates had been having a last tuck into their stocks of food and wine. An array of interesting bottles of brandy had been left lying around and as we passed from room to room, I sampled a few – most of them were rather good. I was in good spirits when we got back to camp at 0800.

Finally back at camp, we found that a search party was being organised to come and look for us. The commanding officer summoned me to his office at 0930. I imagined he wanted a report on the tower but it turned out he wanted to offer me a captaincy because our second in command had received a wound in his shoulder from one of the anti–personnel bombs the enemy had scattered during the night. I immediately declined the offer – I'd just had the most exciting three days of my life. But I knew in my heart that I should accept and, within a few minutes, I did just that.

Thinking how lucky it was that we had not been challenged, and mindful that Sten guns were notoriously unreliable, I was determined to make sure mine worked properly. So, the morning after the capture of the tower I found an empty piece of ground and fired into some bushes. A soldier stood up in front of me.

'What the hell are you doing? You almost took my effing head off, Sir!'
During the morning of D-Day plus four our Number 2 Platoon built two more 80ft Bailey bridges over the Orne River and the canal. One had to be completed before the other was started but both were finished by 1100.

By D-Day plus six we had hot showers rigged at our headquarters, which were used by most of the troops in our area. I opened a demonstration room to display the various types of enemy mines we had found. It was a fearsome collection. By D-Day plus ten there was an air of normality about our base. Somebody was playing the piano I had rescued from the bunker – rather well – and Mademoiselle Madeleine (in spite of the fact that her mother had been killed by our bombers the day before we landed) was giving French lessons in the evenings to enthusiastic classes. And mail was getting through from home. That was a real bonus, and it was so good to hear from Nancy. Of course, I could not tell her much because of censorship. The Army even printed cards for us to send home with just enough room to scribble, 'with much love, Bob'. In due course I was asked to remove my 'mine museum' – they were all still 'live' and next to our billet blocks.

As I mentioned, in the end we stayed in Ouistreham for over a month. Apart from the shelling, it was a pleasant enough place and we were kept very busy throughout. The great gale which blew for three days from June 18 to 21 put both Mulberry harbours out of action and our men spent a great deal of time helping repair the Mulberry at Arromanches. The American Mulberry never reopened. But, for the most part, our unit was engaged in water supply – we had sunk several well points and were soon supplying water to all our forces – and keeping our roadways in good order. Mine clearance was, as always, a priority. Part of my job was to look for accommodation with good cover and places for transport where our blokes could stay as a group. One day going a little south of Ouistreham, I stopped to speak to one of our soldiers standing by the side of the road.

'Any Jerry around here?' I asked him.
'Yes, in the house just round the corner.'
I drove straight back to our unit from whence I had come.

As time went on, I guess we all began to get rather worried about what appeared to be a stalemate between the Allied and German armies. We recognised that the Allies held the initiative but we were all aware of the severe casualties being suffered by our fighting troops, including our Canadian friends. While we had little real idea of the overall position, it seemed to us that if our troops could not get to Caen, just a few miles south, we were likely to be in France for the rest of the year. There were, however, many good reasons to hope for the best, and our air power was fantastic.

Shortly after we had become stationed in Ouistreham, our Commanding Officer began to realise that the local people had experienced a bad time under the Germans and consequently they were, not unreasonably, wary of the new military presence of our own troops in their town. My Commanding Officer made a point of asking me how we could help alleviate the fears of the local population. Perhaps we could find out any things they needed help with, like repairs to their roads or housing; all our Engineers were keen to help. Our piano came to the rescue and in the local village hall we organised the first of what were to become many future parties.

Our unit was fortunate in that we sustained very few casualties and there was always plenty of good and useful work for us to do. Morale was high and our piano played its part. I wrote a songbook, got it roughly copied and we all enjoyed singing together. I had a good, strong voice but I did have some critics, including my father, safe at home in Bury, who told me I did not always sing in tune. We held quiz nights, concerts and dances and made everyone welcome, taking care to make friends with our French neighbours. Madeleine was always a help if we ran into difficulties here.

In fact, the piano became a very important part of our strange lives. In our early days in Ouistreham, our little get-togethers around the piano, often with some of the French locals, encouraged friendship where once fear had reigned.

I often wondered about the background of the German officer who had brought this piano to the Normandy coast in the hope of seeing out the last few months of the war with some 'cultural home comforts'. I am sure he had hoped that his piano music would have helped him while away the time towards what would surely be an eventual German victory; or so his own propaganda told him.

These were times when we made the best of friends quickly, bonded by a common purpose, and although there were long periods of inactivity there were often times of high adventure and danger. Great friends and great adventure – what more could a young man want?

It soon became something of a ritual amongst our men that every Saturday evening, whatever we were doing, we would make sure we would have a song or two around the piano, inviting locals maybe for a drink or two, if there was any to be had, and occasionally even a dance. It didn't matter how near the frontline we were, it was something we looked forward to every week and our piano gave us something small to look forward to – a real morale booster.

The Breakout, as it was called, did not take place until July 25. After that date everything progressed at bewildering speed. Part of the German Army suffered a crushing defeat at Falaise, just a few miles south of where we were stationed, and after that their army seemed to melt away. Then, together with our Allies, we were all on the move and in less than three weeks our unit was on the banks of the Seine. Having spent so much time close to Caen, which had now been razed to the ground, we could scarcely believe it. Once there, our field company built a Bailey bridge, which made me very proud. It spanned the Seine in front of Rouen Cathedral at a point where the river is very wide, requiring three spans. The whole job was completed in 48 hours. The bridge was an all-out team effort: our sergeant major, latrine men, chefs, drivers, officers – the lot – all carrying panels to get the bridge finished on time. It was a marvellous bridge, which stood proud for more than 20 years and was used by everyone, soldiers and civilians alike. When the bridge had been built I remember falling asleep in a chair and thinking about Nancy while someone played our piano, beautifully.

4

Arnhem And The Far East

It seemed that no sooner had we built our marvellous bridge across the Seine that I was ordered to go on ahead with our engineer's advance party to Nijmegen, a town close to Arnhem in Holland. Once there, I was instructed to find suitable premises to billet our corps when it arrived after travelling across France. At that time there was a feeling that the war might soon be over. There was no denying that things were going rather well, with the Allied advance sweeping across Europe, but I was not so sure. I knew how hard the Germans had fought round Caen and I could not believe things would be any different when we got closer to the Nazi homeland.

Several times our road on the way to Nijmegen was cut, presumably by enemy troops left behind our lines during the Allies' rapid advance, and it was slow going, with heavy and congested traffic on narrow roads. I had no doubt, however, that it would be worse for our guys as they followed us with the corps' heavy equipment. We knew little of what was going on but understood there was to be a major offensive of some kind, presumably through Holland. Why else was our corps to be stationed in Nijmegen? On arrival, I negotiated with the town's burgermeister and it was agreed that we might take over their technical college, not that we ever did. As usual in war, there was a last-minute change of plan.

From my experience at Ouistreham I knew that speed was of the essence and it was a great coup that the bridge over the River Waal at Nijmegen had been captured and secured by the Guards Armoured Division. But within days it was to have a hole blown through its centre by two German frogmen swimming down the river from upstream with explosives. Remarkably, our corps completed the repair within 48 hours by spanning the hole with Bailey bridging. We were a very efficient unit and proud of our expertise.

In later years, I was to learn more about the German frogmen from an elderly Dutch dentist, who had been practising in Holland during the war. He treated a few Germans and remembered one patient in particular. Towards the end of the war, a member of the German Navy, an experienced diver, had asked for his help. Diving to any depth can sometimes affect the teeth if there are pockets of air in the cavities. His teeth were in poor condition. He told the dentist that he and another diver had been charged with blowing up the main bridge at Nijmegen to try to halt the Allied advance. This was to be done by entering the river from the German side upstream and taking with them a small raft packed with explosive charges, designed to blow upwards and take out one of the main spans. The subsequent explosion was a spectacular success and left a huge gaping hole in the centre of the bridge. The frogman, with great difficulty, made his way back to his own lines despite the loss of his companion who was killed by Allied fire. Back with his unit, the diver was shown the results of his work by aerial reconnaissance. Sure enough there was a huge hole in the middle of the bridge. But, incredibly, that hole had already been spanned by a Bailey highway. The frogman told the dentist that when he saw the repair had been done so quickly, he knew that Germany would lose the war.

What can I tell you about the Battle for Arnhem? It was a very confusing affair, even for those of us who were there. Ultimately, it was a tragic and extremely bloody battle, which saw many good men – airborne troops and soldiers – killed or wounded by a superior German force. Few had expected that two Panzer divisions would be in the close vicinity. Those two German divisions outgunned the Allies and controlled the battle almost from the start.

General Montgomery's plans for the Battle of Arnhem (as they were later revealed) had been relatively simple. We would strike at the German forces through Holland, an easier target, Montgomery thought, than attacking the German defences behind the River Rhine and the Siegfried Line. Then, if the attack was successful, we could out-flank those defensive positions. But it was a big 'if'. The codename for the Battle of Arnhem was 'Operation Market Garden'. Later, it became better known as 'A Bridge Too Far'.

The battle started on Sunday, September 17 with a heavy bombardment of the German defences followed by an airlift which, over three days, landed more than 30,000 British and American troops whose mission was to capture the eight bridges that spanned the network of canals and rivers on the Dutch/German border. Some of the parachutists drifted off target by a few miles but most landed in good order and, having gathered up their equipment, began to move towards the bridges they had to take. But even at that early stage there was an unexpected level of resistance from the German forces. One British battalion managed to find its way through the German perimeter round Arnhem and by 2000 hours on the first day had captured the northern end of its road bridge, which crossed the Rhine. The Americans, too, reached their objectives, but most of the bridges were blown up before they could be captured.

All in all, overall progress on the first day was reasonable. However, the Germans had been bringing in reinforcements and their Panzers, already stationed nearby, unbeknown to British Intelligence, were moving into Arnhem ready to take on the lightly armed British Paratroopers. On the third day, American troops reached Nijmegen Bridge and were ordered to attack across the River Waal and capture the German end. The firing was so intense that it looked like a hailstorm as bullets hit the river and kicked up little spouts of water. More than half the men in the company making the attack were killed or wounded but the survivors successfully stormed the bridge and the route to Arnhem was now in Allied hands. It was a costly victory.

It was, however, by then too late for the British Parachute Battalion at the north end of Arnhem Bridge. The Germans had moved their tanks into the town and, one by one, had demolished the houses in which the British had been fighting. Our paratroopers had few anti-tank weapons, no food and, crucially, little ammunition. The attack had failed and there was nothing for it but to get as many of our troops as possible back across the river. Market Garden proved to be a disaster and it would be another four months before the Allies would once again attempt to cross the Rhine. There was honour in the defeat – the Allies fought with great courage over a long period – but the numbers of comrades killed and seriously wounded were hard to comprehend and harder still to bear. The British 1st Airborne Division suffered losses of 1,174 killed in action and 5,903 captured or missing. There are many theories as to why things went so wrong at Arnhem. Faulty Intelligence? Perhaps. Nobody seemed to have expected there to be two Panzer divisions, or had good advice been ignored? Was the plan just too optimistic? Probably. I think that Montgomery and his generals had failed to appreciate the difficulty of fighting in a built-up area with narrow roads, sometimes with a canal alongside. Territory of this kind is much easier to defend than attack.

My corps stayed in Nijmegen for the whole of that winter. During our stay we established an auxiliary floating bridge, a Bailey bridge around two-thirds of a mile long, made up of separate 100ft spans held in place by barges. It was to be used as an alternative in case the main bridge became damaged or inoperable.

It was a long winter and our posting for so many months at Nijmegen was no rest cure. From time to time we would be under irregular mortar fire from the German border town of Kleve but we still had our piano, and morale, despite the Arnhem defeat, was pretty good. And then, out of the blue, I had a remarkable piece of luck. To my astonishment, on January 11, 1945 I won a lottery for a week's leave through a scheme known as 'Monty's Weekend'. I returned immediately to England and to Christchurch, where, much to my relief, Nancy accepted my proposal and we became engaged. It was marvellous to see her again, although the matron at her hospital was very reluctant to give Nancy any extra time off from her duties. But that was just the way things were in those days.

Back in Nijmegen it was a cold winter, and our bridge – it was a floating bridge, remember – became a barrier for pack ice, which tended to jam up in front of the bridge end and, of course, in front of the various barges on which the bridge had been built. It became a great problem and there was a real possibility that we might lose the bridge until someone had the bright idea of enlisting the help of specialist loggers from the Canadian troops. It worked a treat. The Canadians used their art of dancing along floating logs to position booms to guide the ice through waterways between the boats. As you might imagine, it was a tricky operation but remarkably, after a short spell of training from the Canadians, our chaps could do the job almost as well as they did.

During our time in Holland we got to know the Dutch people pretty well. They were short of food and I think they had probably suffered even worse conditions under the German occupation than those endured by the French, but the citizens round Arnhem offered our troops great assistance without being asked – nursing their wounds and often hiding some of them in their homes, at great personal risk.

Two incidents in particular during that long, cold winter I still remember well. One day I saw a pall of smoke in the sky. I knew some of our chaps were out clearing mines. 'Oh God,' I thought, 'that's Sergeant Estie', and it was. When I got there I saw Estie's group had indeed been defusing enemy mines. One of them had had a different type of fuse to those they were used to dealing with and, sadly, the thing had gone off, killing several of our corps. It was a bad day and felt especially harsh as, just a fortnight earlier, one of our bridge loading parties had been hit by a shell. In those two incidents we had casualties of 19 and 20 respectively, more than our corps had suffered throughout the entire campaign. None of us enjoyed that winter in Holland, and we mourned the loss of our comrades. Most of Holland was cut off and food became increasingly scarce. Many people died and some were reduced to eating bulbs to survive.

As for the piano, I found out long after the war that our customary Saturday evening sing-song had continued, along with the piano, right through to Berlin. This had proved to be not only a great morale booster for our troops, but often also a link with the local people and a blessed relief for them from the horrors of war. I have often wondered what happened to the piano or indeed it's rightful owner. Where, I wonder, is that German officer now? I would love to meet him and return his piano.

We knew that by the end of the winter there would be a push across the Rhine. To that end we had instructions to move upstream to Kleve and build another bridge there. While we were being geared up for that operation, experienced 'volunteers' were needed go out to the Far East to take part in a beach landing in Malaya. Well, having won one lottery, I could hardly expect to win another. I was volunteered and there was not much I could do about it.

Towards the end of March I was given a month's embarkation leave and on March 31 Nancy and I were married at Christchurch Priory, with Nancy making most of the arrangements at very short notice. It was a wonderful day and the Bailey boys did us proud, providing a uniformed guard of honour, not with swords but with rifles and bayonets. I took Nancy on a honeymoon to the Lake District and then on to meet my family in Tottington. They loved her instantly, as I knew they would, and we had a very happy time. It took Nancy a little while to get used to my family's broad Lancashire accents, but she felt entirely at home and laughed at their jokes – it was a good start to our marriage.

Time flashed by and Nancy had just ten days leave before she had to return to her hospital duties. But somehow in that precious month I found time to take my final civil engineering exams. All too soon, my leave was over. Nancy and I both prayed that Japan would be defeated and that I would be home before too long. My troop ship sailed from Southampton on May 2. It was a large ship, shabby but reasonably clean. I cannot say I liked life on board – for some reason I have always been a little distrustful of the sea, more so since my D-day experience. The officers' quarters were comfortable enough and, of course, there were great celebrations on board when VE Day finally arrived. It had been a long time coming. I could only hope that my colleagues of the 31st Beach Group had got through the last months of the war without any more casualties. I found myself missing my old friends and the piano. I was told later that the piano had ended up in Berlin. It had continued to be a good friend and morale booster to all our troops. It would be good to think that it found a good home and is still being played.

The Japanese surrendered on August 16. We didn't know the details; all we knew was that an atomic bomb – an American super-bomb – had forced the Japanese to surrender. I was delighted and thought it wonderful that just a couple of bombs could bring the whole ghastly war to an end. At that time I had no sense of the full extent of the atomic bomb's destructive force. I just thought (wrongly, as it later turned out) 'what a fantastic weapon!' As it happened, our corps was in transit camp at the time of the surrender, waiting to be landed in Malaya. The operation went ahead – nobody, it seemed, could stop it. We landed on Morey beach, near Port Swetnam, where the Japanese were in the process of surrendering. There was no fighting.

It was just as well there was no fighting because our landing was a shambles. Many of our ships were bogged down on runnels of sand, which stretched the better part of a mile out to sea. It was a very slow business getting our men to the shore. I was on one of the smaller landing craft and we all had to get out and push. It would have been slaughter if the landing had been opposed.

There were few problems when we finally got ashore with little or no Japanese resistance, and we had plenty of time to explore Malaya, an interesting and beautiful country with gentle people. While there, I had the good fortune to meet up with a friend from basic training. We had a competition to see who could find the most interesting things that the Japanese had left behind – in particular, Japanese Samurai swords (carried by their officers) were a real prize. My friend got hold of one but the best I could do was to find a large reel of super-strong red silk Japanese parachute cord, which I later used for many years for jobs around the house and garden.

We had fun, but it all came to a very sad end. One day we found an abandoned miniature glider that could be towed by a jeep or something similar to above the height of the trees. This was how the Japanese had carried out military spotting for artillery. While having a go on the glider, my friend was killed in a tragic accident. Some months later, it was my sad duty to take a small collection of his belongings, including the sword, back home to his family.

At the time, I thought we spent too long in Malaya and that it was all a bit of a waste of time. But, looking back, we did some good work for the country. Malaya had a basic road network, which had been upgraded by the Japanese. The road network was, of course, important for the future of the country, and our corps made many repairs to it. We also carried out an exercise to establish whether or not the main road running north to south on the Malayan peninsular was safe for heavy-duty traffic. It needed to be classified. The Top Brass must have said: 'We need to test the bridges. Let's get someone to drive a fully loaded tank transporter across them; now who do we know silly enough to do that?' Needless to say, I was given the job of upgrading all the bridges between Kuala Lumpur and Butterworth, the main route through Malaya. It was felt by the authorities that it should be a Class 18 route and the best way to ensure this would be to take an 18-ton load with half a dozen Indian troops and drive the length of the road, making an assessment of the bridges as we went. We took it very slowly to begin with and effected repairs with timber and bits of steel where needed as we went along. Some were floating bridges and we had to make a reasonable engineering assessment as to whether each could take the load and then we would take our 18 tons across at increasing speeds. If it didn't collapse, it was a Class 18 bridge. I remember we did have a bit of trouble with our last bridge, near Butterworth, which was a floating bridge. Water started rushing into its supporting boats as we crossed. I had to make a report about that.

One thing I found very interesting was that when we tested local materials to see how good they were, some of the hardwoods were very much stronger than the timber we used at home. Indeed, some of the breaking strengths were near the working strength of steel. One wood in particular, which, if memory serves me right, was called Changain Arabu, was quite remarkable in this respect.

In September 1945, I was promoted to Major but it meant little to me, as there was nothing I wanted more than to return to civilian life and my new wife. Soldiering was not the kind of life I wanted any longer, and the sooner I got back to a normal and a useful existence the better. But I had to wait until March 1946 before I caught a troop ship heading for home.

5

Home Sweet Home

I was as excited as a schoolboy when our elderly troop ship docked in Southampton and there was Nancy, standing almost alone on the quayside in a red hat and her best coat. What a cheer she got from the hundreds of our lads leaning over the guard rails. Somehow she had got information as to the arrival time of our ship, which no one else seemed to know. Embarrassed by the cheers and some ribald comments, she blushingly retired to a waiting room. Rescuing her, I thought I was the luckiest man in the world.

It was so good to see Nancy; it had been over a year since I last saw her. Within in a few days we were heading north to Tottington and a new life together. Of course, Tottington had changed and was not quite the place I remembered. Our family house in Booth Street had been sold after my mother's death and the closure of Walshaw Mill, so there was nothing for it but to move in with dad. Our first home turned out to be three rooms on the top floor of his wholesale tobacconist shop, plumb in the centre of Bury. Fortunately, Nancy and my dad got on rather well, despite his vivid stories of strike-breaking and how he dealt with one of his employees, a Mr Isherwood, by knocking him over several looms. My father had never been the easiest of men; he had decided views and opinions and could be downright rude. But Nancy would laugh at his jokes, even the bad ones, and somehow the two of them got on.

My priority was to get back to work and I have to say that the staff at Tottington Urban District Council made me very welcome when I returned to my old job. I was responsible for designing and building new public facilities and housing schemes for my home town, which included a new public toilet. I was very lucky to walk straight back into my old job, but Tottington was a very small town and I needed promotion and a better-paid position if I was going to make a living which would be sufficient to support Nancy and the family we hoped we might soon have.

Nancy settled into Tottington well. Initially, she had some difficulty understanding the local accents, but she soon got over that and thought people friendlier in the North than they were in the South. Just occasionally I would go for one of my long, solitary walks into the

Pennines, where I had once prided myself on being able to pinpoint exactly where I was by accents of the local people. But now I found I was not so sure and I was pleased to get home. Times were changing and so was I, but on the surface things were much the same, despite the country's new Labour government. Dad was outraged – he would, he told everyone, vote for a pig if it was a Conservative. He was overheard telling one of his friends that his son had married a communist. Actually, I shared some of my dad's Conservative values but I had strong Labour sympathies, too. I made it a rule that I would never discuss politics while I was working for a council. I thought it very important to remain neutral.

We didn't stay long in Bury. In 1947, we moved when I got a job I had seen advertised for an engineer in Swindon, Wiltshire, which included one of the new post-war prefabricated houses, known as prefabs. Nancy and I were delighted – a home of our own. It was fun putting our little house in good order and planting the garden. It was while we were living in Swindon that our much-loved daughter, Christine, was born at the John Radcliffe Hospital in Oxford. I had approached a rather elderly local doctor to ask whether I should use the new National Health Service.

'Oh no, it will never last,' he told me.

And so I paid for Nancy to go to Oxford. All went well and she came back with a lovely baby daughter. I was very proud.

The winter of 1947 was the coldest for many years and I could not help but be reminded of the winter I had spent in Nijmegen with my corps of engineers. It had been so cold there that even the River Waal had frozen and great lumps of ice would rush down the river and crash into our closely guarded bridge. At one time it seemed that the bridge itself might be swept away. I had never known such cold. But I had survived the cold, the war and all its dangers. I reflected on how lucky I had been when so many others had been maimed or killed. Among those were my friend Sergeant Estie and his group, who had been killed defusing a new German mine, and our colonel, who had been shot and killed on the Nijmegen Bridge just a few days after I had left for my embarkation leave to Malaya. I didn't want to think about the war – it was over but sometimes, without warning, memories would return.

Our second child, our son Robert, was born just before we made another move, this time to Doncaster, where I had secured a new and better-paid job as an engineering assistant. We called Robert 'Robin' for some years. I can't remember why, but either name made a break in the family tradition of naming the grandson after the grandfather. Nancy had refused to consider Fred, my dad's name. She said it was inappropriate for her son. Was it too common perhaps, or had she and Fred had a tiff? I never knew the answer.

Our next move was to Doncaster. We were excited, especially with our new home – a brand new semi-detached house on the A1. Of course, there was more than enough traffic on that busy road, but back then it was only a trickle compared with what it is today. It was a happy house and we made very good friends with a family who lived just a few doors away. One day, when Christine was little more than a toddler, their little boy came round to our house and asked if she would like to play football. It is the kind of thing one remembers. We had lots of parties – for Christmas, birthdays and for no other reason than we just felt like one. Food was still rationed but people were kind to us newcomers and were always asking if we had enough for our babies. For myself, I enjoyed working for Doncaster Council, despite it being rather an odd collection of Yorkshiremen.

It was in Doncaster that I first took Nancy to the races. A painter who was helping us decorate our new house gave Nancy a tip: Black Tarquin to win the St Leger. So we went on our bikes to the racecourse. The race itself was like an old-fashioned cavalry charge – colourful and exciting – and, to add to the fun, our horse won by a head or a neck – I'm not sure which – but we returned home with more money than we had started out with. On the Monday we thanked the painter, who was rather subdued and told us he hadn't backed the horse.

'Why not?' we asked.

'Well, it wouldn't have been right. I was not supposed to tell anybody.'

Yes, Doncaster was a real success, both for me and for our family, and we were all sorry to leave. Perhaps sensing that we were going to leave, young Robert took it into his head, at the age of 18 months, to crawl from one side of the A1 to the other, giving us the fright of our lives.

Our third move was back to Bury. I was slowly climbing the borough engineers' 'executive ladder' and this time I was appointed Bury's Assistant Borough Engineer. For this move, I was able to buy a house, a large Victorian semi-detached in Bury New Road. Christine loved the house, with it playroom, its sweeping staircase and stained-glass windows, and, of course, the solid fuel Rayburn, which kept us warm. And the fields behind the house were open and free for us to roam – a real bonus.

Sadly, after we moved to Bury, we had difficulties at home. When Jonathan, our second son, was born Nancy was very ill and took a long time to recover. Ethel, Nancy's mother, came to stay with us to help out. It would have been a difficult enough job for her at the best of times and things became rather fraught. But it was kind of Ethel to help us, and I am sure I did not make things any easier by being very busy at work. But the crisis passed and soon our Christine had started school at Elm Street Primary and I had bought my first car, an Austin A30. Nancy was still a bit weak from her illness but growing stronger, and I enjoyed taking her out in my new motor. It was still quite something to own a car in those days.

It was while we were in Bury that I began to take a real interest in the characters of our children. Christine was a lovely child, anxious to please, careful and hardworking. Robert was a worrier and a poor sleeper, but he was still very young and he was a lovely lad. Somehow I knew he would do well. And then there was Jon, full of mischief and always in a hurry, it seemed, to get on with life. Like Fred in a way – a bit of a card – but from his open face and smile, I knew we would always be friends.

I thought we were settled for a while in Bury, but in 1956 we were on the move back to Yorkshire, this time to Harrogate, a marvellous town with a green that extended into its very heart. It was another promotion, but another move meant more hard work for Nancy, and I realised that all this moving around would become more difficult as the children got older and had to change schools. I found myself worrying whether the new school we had found for Christine would be good for her. Nevertheless, I really enjoyed my new job and to be deputy to the borough engineer in a place as important as Harrogate was indeed a promotion.

Politics aside – the town was dyed-in-the-wool Conservative – Nancy and I loved Harrogate, and we set our hearts on a property that was being offered for sale by auction. In addition to the house, there were two fields and some outbuildings. We thought our bid would be accepted but, to our disappointment, we were outbid by the Great Yorkshire Show, which wanted the fields for car parking during the few days a year when the show was on. Still, in the end I managed to rent the house – a five-bedroomed detached property – and half an acre of land, including the outbuildings, for just £200 per year. Such a deal was still possible in the 1960s.

During our stay in Harrogate, Martin, our third and much-loved son, was born. Thankfully, all went well with mother and child, very much to my relief as after Jon's birth Nancy had been warned of possible difficulties should she have more children. Nancy and I have been blessed with a marvellous family.

Our time in Harrogate, like our time in Doncaster, was very happy. I always seemed to be short of money but we had fun and a donkey called Molly. Molly was a nice, gentle beast but she did have a habit of wandering off and she certainly had a mind of her own. I had great fun building the donkey's stable. Every year we had a very large party during the Great Yorkshire Show, when dad would arrive with a bunch of singers. Nancy, as always, was a marvellous host.

Harrogate seemed too good a place to leave but then I saw a new job advertised: A chief borough engineer was required in Maidstone, Kent. I had to try for a top job and so, once again, I tossed my hat into the ring.

6

Rebuilding Maidstone

It was in December 1959 that I was appointed Borough Engineer for Maidstone but my job did not start officially until April 1960. I was 41 and was delighted, not only with the job but with the prospect of being in charge. A bit conceited perhaps, but I had been working all my adult life toward that end. The years of working for Tottington, Doncaster, Swindon, Harrogate and, of course, Bury councils had been my training, as had my time in the Army, which had taught me how to manage and lead people. I felt I was ready for the job and was determined to make the most of the opportunity and do my best for the people of Maidstone. Nancy and I would miss Harrogate, we always would, and I could not help but wonder how Molly the donkey would fare without us.

Within a few days of our arrival in Maidstone we had bought our next home, Pickering Cottage in Pickering Street. I remember the day well – it was very cold and snowy, as it can sometimes be in Kent, the closest county in England to the Continent. The house suited us, although its name was deceptive – it was much grander and larger than a cottage. The exterior had a Georgian look and there was an impressive circular drive leading to the front door. There were five bedrooms, an extensive garden, a tennis court and, immediately next door, a Scout hut, very handy for our three boys. Unusually, it was a house that was almost entirely made of wood and I wondered for an anxious day or two if we would get a mortgage. We soon found out that Pickering Cottage had an interesting history. It had previously been the home of Admiral and Lady Keyes. Admiral Keyes had been a war hero who had first served on the China Station and then in different capacities throughout both world wars. He had witnessed the shameful defeat in the Dardanelles and, by all accounts, there is little doubt that had he been in command the result could have been very different. His next appointment had been to captain the battleship HMS Centurion, part of the British North Sea Fleet, which, just a few months earlier, had defeated the Germans in the Battle of Jutland. I say defeated the Germans, but was it a victory? Some say it was more of a draw. Nevertheless, the German Navy never managed to break the blockade of their ports and that was a decisive factor in our winning the First World War.

The admiral's next job had been to plan the daring and successful attack on Zeebrugge and its submarine pens in January 1918. The Prime Minister, Lloyd George, was driven down from London to discuss the matter with Admiral Keyes and I liked to imagine his Rolls Royce parked on our circular drive. I did find it rather curious that Lloyd George should come from London personally to interview Keyes but I have since learned that, following the grievous loss of life in France and the mistakes made, Lloyd George had an inherent distrust of the Army generals. There can be little doubt that this distrust would have extended to Naval admirals – they, too, had let the country down through their lack of resolve over the Dardanelles and the absence of a clear-cut victory at Jutland. In any event and whatever the reason (although, thinking about it, what better place could there be to judge a man than in his own home?) the meeting went well. Lloyd George supported the plan and the raid proved to be one of the most successful operations of the entire war.

When Keyes was eventually retired after the First World War he became Member of Parliament for Portsmouth, and it was in the House of Commons that he performed his last great service for King and Country. Appalled by the fiasco of Britain's invasion of Norway, and dressed in full uniform decorated with his medals, he made a devastating speech to the House about the loss of the Ark Royal and what had gone wrong with the Norway campaign. Two days later, Prime Minister Neville Chamberlain resigned and Winston Churchill took his place.

Lady Keyes, too, was a remarkable person, employing miners to tend her fruit trees, which covered much of Pickering and the village of Loose. It was a welcome change for the miners, so very different from the wretched and dirty job of mining underground. It is said that Lady Keyes was also instrumental in finding miners other work, including the building and repair of sea walls. Jon, my son, was later to examine a sea wall that miners had built near Brighton and wrote about their work. He considered their craftsmanship extremely good.

I got down to work immediately at the council. Looking back, I realise I spent rather more time at the office than I should have. I have always been particular and hardworking (a trait inherited from my family?) and was perhaps over-anxious that others might make mistakes and fail to follow my instructions. But we had a happy home life. Nancy was a superb host and homemaker, and I worked hard at making our family holidays and free time fun. In that respect, my children tell me, I succeeded. And, of course, I enjoyed our activity holidays just as much as the rest of the family, probably more. Taking the family walking and rambling through the Lake District was as near to heaven as I could imagine. What would we see when we crested the next hill and would the mist clear for us to catch a glimpse of the sea? When we had been in Maidstone for two years, my dad moved 'down south', as he said, to be near us, bringing, to my great joy, Aunt Rachel with him. We found them a nice little house 200 yards down the road from Pickering Cottage and everything worked rather well, with the children coming and going between us and their grandfather as they wished. Sadly, our children's maternal grandmother, Ethel – Nancy's mum – died peacefully at our home in 1966. For some years her health had been in decline but she had always done her best for us. She had lived with us since moving in when Nancy was so very poorly. I am sure Ethel enjoyed her time with the Orrells, just as we enjoyed having her, but I know she found our growing family and me, her son-in-law, sometimes a little too hot to handle.

I could never say that my work was too onerous at Maidstone, and I much enjoyed the challenge, but the hours could be long and difficult for family life, especially as council meetings were often held in the evenings. And then there were the periodic emergencies when the river Medway would burst its banks and there would be sewage to deal with as well as flooding. Heavy snow was another problem.

Maidstone is an old town – it was established in the 15th century – but its importance as a trading centre for agricultural produce had long gone by the time we arrived. The so-called Garden of England was still producing good stuff but there were quicker ways of getting its produce to London than by barge. So a large part of my job was to try to help make Maidstone into a modern town and create new jobs. Of course, this was all very political and I was continually surprised at how often council members would say one thing and do another. I stuck to my principles and remained strictly neutral. That being said, I became a Rotarian, and Nancy and I took an interest in a number of local organisations, including the Scouts and their splendid gang shows.

When I look back I am surprised, pleased and rather proud of how much my department, admittedly with help from others, achieved during my 14 years in charge. We built a new library, new swimming baths and the first stage of a better road system, with plans for the second stage. We built 2,547 new houses and three multi-storey blocks of flats, together with car parks and shopping centres. We wanted to make sure that Maidstone maintained its position as Kent's county town, so its retail side was very important. We also needed to look to the future and encourage new jobs, so we developed an industrial estate at Park Wood.

Some 14 years after I arrived in Maidstone, a governmental re-organisation decreed that the town no longer required a borough engineer and surveyor. I was, of course, upset and, if I am honest, rather bitter at losing my job but I was treated with such great kindness by so many in the town that, on occasion, I was moved almost to tears. Of course, I did not cry. That would never have done – I was still a Lancashire man after all.

My farewell to civic life in Maidstone culminated in a party I thought I was holding for my staff, friends and family at the Royal Star Hotel. But the party had been hijacked. A little way into the festivities, I found myself on stage and subject to a 'This Is Your Life' event – many of you will remember the television series, originally hosted by Eamonn Andrews. My administrative assistant, Geoff Jeans, stood in for Mr Andrews, acting as master of ceremonies. He ran the proceedings so well I wondered why I had not noticed his latent talent. As you can imagine, it was a very emotional evening for me, with so many old friends travelling long distances to be there. In particular, it was marvellous to see Ronald Taylor (by then a director of British Steel) who had been such a friend when I arrived at the Experimental Bridging Establishment in Christchurch. As I've already told you, I had just come out of hospital and was still an invalid who found it difficult to walk in a straight line. But Ronald took me in hand and introduced me to Nancy. What more could I have asked of him?

All my family, including my first granddaughter, Caroline, were at the celebration. All my family, that is, except for my son, Robert, who was studying and working. But Robert sent me a tape-recorded message. At the end of the evening, after the Town Clerk, Trevor Scholes, and Alderman, Sir Gordon Larkin, had paid their tributes, I realised that most of those whom I had I had met or had dealings with in Maidstone were sad to see me go. That was a compliment that touched my heart.

Our family's 14 years in Maidstone had gone in a flash. Nancy and I had been very happy and so, too, had our children, except perhaps for Jonathan, who found life difficult. Mind you, he had his faults – he could be wilful and always thought he knew best. But he was loyal and generous at heart and had talents, such as the ability to draw and play musical instruments. By the time I retired from Maidstone Council, Jon had left home and, while I worried about him, I kind of knew he would be all right. As always, there were other concerns. I began to be worried about my father, fearing that he might be beginning to suffer from dementia. But while some of his behaviour had of late been rather odd, I comforted myself with the thought that it always had been.

In many ways, March 1974 was the end of an era for Nancy and me. Our children were, for all practical purposes, grown up. Two were at university, and only Martin was still at school. I was really proud of them and that included Jon, who was still something of a loose cannon and had started work at 16. So what next? Well, the first thing I had to do was to get a job. Despite living in a splendid house with a circular drive, we had little money in the bank and little spare to support our children should they need help. My experience in planning came to the rescue. A month after I had left Maidstone Council I secured a job vetting planning appeals for Tonbridge and District in Kent. A little to my surprise, I much enjoyed the new job but wondered what the morrow might bring.

7

Retirement And A Return To Christchurch

I could have carried on working for the new local authority in Kent. I thought about it and would have liked to finish the work I had started, but change was in the air, not only for Maidstone but for the country. Reorganisation, so popular with politicians, was not always for the best, and big was not always beautiful. There were other things that troubled me: rabid commercialism was affecting all our lives and anything for a quick buck seemed to be the order of the day. The salaries paid to high earners, some of whom were little more than gamblers, had grown out of all proportion. And now there was big trouble with the miners. Where would it all end?

Perhaps I was too cynical. There was no doubt that most people were better off, better fed and better cared for than they had been before the war. For myself, I found that I was enjoying my new job working on planning appeals for Tonbridge. I found it interesting and challenging mentally, a welcome change from the work I had been doing for the better part of 30 years. It is said that change can be as good as a rest; it was for me.

At Pickering Cottage life, too, was changing for Nancy and me. The house was so quiet. All our children had left home and we missed them terribly. But, despite their busy lives, they all kept in touch and in that we were very fortunate. I had persuaded Jon to get a job with McAlpine, who would give him day release to study. He would disappear for long periods, working in Scotland and on the North Sea oil rigs, a dangerous and demanding job, but I knew he would make good in the end. Robert and Martin were now doctors, doing important and responsible jobs, and Christine, who had done very well at university, was a teacher.

The most pressing problem we had to deal with after my retirement was what, if anything, I could do to help my father. Unhappily, there was simply no doubt that he was suffering from dementia and that it was getting worse by the day. It is a cruel affliction that can be as bad for the carers as for the sufferers. Rachel tried so very hard to keep my dad in some kind of order but there was nothing she could do. Dad was still strong, determined and sometimes violent. We tried putting him in several nursing homes but none could cope and in the end he had to be sent to a secure unit. It was a sad end for a remarkable man, who throughout his life had the priceless ability to make people laugh and enjoy themselves. Despite his faults, I loved him dearly.

After my father had died in such distressing circumstances, I was heartened when Aunt Rachel came to live with us. She was great company for both of us and, in particular, for Nancy, who had been feeling rather lonely. I sometimes wondered why Rachel had never married. She liked men, I was sure of that, and anybody who could put up with Fred for so many years had to be kind and tolerant. I guess the reason why she remained a spinster is that she never had the fortune to meet the right man. It was, of course, the same for hundreds of thousands of young women living in Britain after the First World War. The slaughter of so many young men in over four years of fighting meant there were not enough of them to go round. It is calculated that in the 1920s and 1930s there were one-and-a-half million more women of marriageable age living in our country than there were men.

Sadly, within two years of my father's death, Rachel, too, had died after being ill for some time. She had been a great friend and confidante for all of us – Nancy, myself and all of our children – and it was difficult to imagine what life would be like without her. But Nancy had nursed her with love and care in our cottage and that gave us all comfort, as we felt in some small way we were repaying the debt we owed her. Sometimes, in the last summer of her life, Rachel would watch from her bedroom as I did the gardening. On those occasions, without even seeing her, I could feel her presence and know that, in some way, it was she who was still caring for me.

After Rachel died it was not unusual to find Nancy and me alone in our cottage for days at a time. We were beginning to consider what we might do with the rest of our lives, which, unbeknown to us then, of course, would prove more of an adventure than either of us could have possibly imagined. But back then we thought about our lives in Maidstone and what we would miss. In particular, we would miss the Scouts and the gang shows, for which Nancy had spent many happy hours preparing costumes while I had helped with the props, once making six helmets out of saucepans. In those days a gang show might well have a cast of 40 or more and be a very professional affair. But slowly and surely they were becoming a thing of the past, another change in life that I would have to accept. While we had made many good friends in Maidstone, we had no real ties. The cottage and garden were becoming too big for us but we would miss Pickering, the special area in which we lived. It still had many fruit trees, which, although no longer farmed, were so beautiful, especially in the spring at blossom time. We used to try to pick some cherries before the birds took the lot. I thought about returning to Manchester but dismissed the idea. There would be nothing there for Nancy or me, except perhaps for a cheaper house and the Lake District in easy reach. Of course, the locals would be kind and friendly, but we both felt our home now lay in the South. After some discussion, the choice became obvious: we would return to Christchurch, the place we had first met. Working for Sir Donald Bailey at Christchurch had been one of the high points of my life. But the move was not just a romantic one – it was the right time and the right place. Nancy still had a brother, Ted, of whom she was very fond, and other friends living in the town.

Did anyone know of a good removal company? We had collected a lot of stuff over the past 18 years.

8

The Costume Gallery

Preparing for our move to Christchurch, I was astonished to find that Nancy had collected some 3,000 costumes, along with many other items: jewellery, umbrellas, hats, swords and shoes. Quite a wardrobe, and her snazzy collection of morning suits could give Moss Bros a run for its money. Many had been made up for the Scouts' gang shows, other stage productions and for fancy dress parties, which had become very popular. I have to say that some of Nancy's costumes were simply wonderful. If somebody wanted to dress up as a policeman, a monkey, a polar bear, Pinocchio or Geppetto the carpenter, Nancy could fix them up in no time at all. She was an excellent and fast-working seamstress who delighted in her work and I was in awe of her talent. She was also very generous and would give away her costumes to those who had difficulty paying. But others, appreciating Nancy for the generous person she was, would make presents of the costumes and clothes they had once worn.

We had no difficulty selling Pickering Cottage. It had been a marvellous family home and it was sad to see it go, but I remembered with a smile how short of money I had been after the initial purchase. My homemade chairs and furniture, some made out of orange boxes, had not been perhaps of quite the standard that people might expect in their borough engineer's house. By the time we moved we had, however, acquired so many possessions that we could not decide whether we would need one removal van or two. Being North Country at heart, I settled on one-and-a-half. Then, with monies paid and house sold, we said goodbye to Maidstone.

I was 60 when we made our move to Christchurch and started an entirely new life. I had, of course, known Nancy's brother, Ted, for some time (it was Ted who had flown Dakotas during the war while I had built bridges) but after the move to Christchurch we became very good friends and had a lot of fun together. One of our first joint ventures was to find a suitable place to store and display Nancy's ever-growing collection of costumes. She reckoned that since my retirement she had made a bit of money from her enterprise but had no real idea about how much or how little that might be. And then, of course, she had a given away a fair few costumes. But, to be fair, Nancy had done very well and both Ted and I were convinced she had a viable business.

But just as important as a home for the costumes was the question of where Nancy and I were going to live. For a while Ted and I had an idea that both our families could share a really nice house, bigger and better than either of us could afford on our own, but nothing came up that fitted the bill and in the end I settled on a smaller house in Wickfield Avenue, which was well placed for the river and the town centre. We found an old workshop down by the river to host Nancy's venture, which she called The Costume Gallery. It was almost derelict and had low headroom but it was dry and the rent was just £800 a year. And so in a very few weeks we had the new breadwinner in our family – Nancy – back in business and for a minimal cost. I found (and I was very pleased with myself) hanging rails and windows at the local scrap yard and our son, Jon, drove over with a friend to help us with the concreting. That called for a few beers and a decent lunch, which Nancy was very happy to provide.

I soon gave in to the family clamour. They were insistent that now I lived so close to a river, I had to get a boat. So I bought a rowing boat, clinker built, very small but very pretty, and called her Caroline, after my first grandchild. In truth I have never really liked boats. Perhaps that first Channel crossing in that wretched landing craft served to put me off. Now and again over the years I would remember the two men we lost overboard on D-Day. I never knew their names. I expect the equipment they were carrying took them straight to the bottom. They never had a chance.

Anyway, to return to the costume business, our temporary gallery was doing very well and the family had much fun sitting round our kitchen table making all kinds of costumes while I helped with props and metal work. Together we did some remarkable work, making an authentic-looking Elizabethan tapestry from thick gouache paint on some old sacking and the head of Mr Punch made from papier maché. We even made a two-man camel with operating eyelids and a mouth.

It soon became apparent that the workshop we had rented was too small for Nancy's business and so with the little bit of money I had left from the sale of Pickering Cottage I bought another house close to the quay. It was in need of refurbishment but had the potential for a decent-sized extension that could be used as a nice showroom and store for our costume gallery. I did the drawings, applied for planning permission and within a few months Ted and I set to work. When it came to the concreting, I was happy enough to allow Jon to give us a hand again. I didn't tell anybody, but I was beginning to feel my age.

Once the new gallery had opened there was an even greater demand for Nancy's costumes, so much so that we had to look for additional help. Nancy found some relatives and friends to give us a helping hand and we did our bit by joining the Youth Training Scheme (YTS). We gave several young people a start through the business. I remember one young man looking at us in complete astonishment when he saw the work we were doing Before long, Nancy had a visit from the taxman. When friends would ask how it was going, Nancy would simply say: 'Well I seem to have a little more money in my purse than I used to.' But, of course, that was not going to wash with the taxman. I wondered how the visit would go. Nancy produced lots and lots of paper – some invoices, some receipts for purchases – and not much else. 'Let's say,' the taxman said at the end of a long interview, 'you are breaking even.' Nancy's charm had won the day.

Nancy and I continued with our costume gallery business for some years and we could always call on Nancy's friends and relatives to help make new costumes for show orders.

All was going well, but there was soon to be a profound change in our lives and, once again, Nancy, in her strange and gentle way, would be the instigator.

9

A World Worth Fighting For

Within a couple of years, Nancy's business was doing very well. To be honest, I had wondered if it would survive the first visit of the taxman. Maybe because Nancy had given so much of the money she had earned to others, the inspector had decided to go easy on her. Then again, there might have been another reason. The inspector must have shuddered at the sight of Nancy's bookkeeping and thought of the task he would face should he challenge the position and have to try to decipher her multitude of various bits of paper, all stuffed into cardboard boxes.

I very much enjoyed working with Ted on the new costume galleries and soon learned that he was a great cartoonist. I was very often the butt of his jokes. Did I really say 'Boogger it!' on the hour? But, when all the building work was finished, I suddenly found myself at a bit of a loose end, which was very unusual for me. I wasn't going to sit and sew, that was women's work (although I was, of course, careful not to voice that particular sentiment) and the garden of our new house could be done in a day. Nevertheless, I kept myself busy. It is curious how gregarious I had become compared to the days of my youth, when I had been something of a loner. Now I loved company and would always find time to have a few beers with a friend.

I started to think about what I might do in the long term: something more serious perhaps, but not necessarily for money. Did I really want to be the town crier? I had done the job on a number of occasions after being 'volunteered' but that was enough. Neither did I want to be a member of the Christchurch Rotary Club. After 12 years service in Maidstone, I had done my bit. But I did volunteer to be the odd-job man for the Burley Youth Hostel and I enjoyed that.

Of course, my first concern in life was to care for Nancy and my children: Christine, Robert, Jon and Martin, together with their growing families. I went to see the children regularly on their own ground, not to interfere in their lives but to enjoy their company and help them, if I could, in an increasingly difficult world. I would go walking with Martin, sometimes in Italy; skiing with Robert and Christine, and would hitch-hike to see Jon in Scotland or wherever he might be living.

I have always had a love of making things and a horror of needless waste. I was, in many ways, an early and committed recycler, who still used the Japanese parachute cord I had found in Malaya in the garden. Sadly, I had never fulfilled my schoolboy ambition and come up with an idea that that would help mankind. The best I achieved was an invention to protect small birds from hungry squirrels pinching their food. I manufactured a squirrel-proof bird feeder made from circular discs of plywood and an upside-down flowerpot with wire mesh. I sold quite a few and gave one to each of my children for Christmas. I cannot remember them thanking me. Maybe my children were on the side of the squirrels.

While I worked in the public sector I had always distanced myself from any of the political parties and I did not much concern myself with the plight of others. But I appreciated that it was fundamental to Nancy's beliefs and very nature to care and even suffer for those who, by accident of birth or war, found difficulty in coping. My main concern was that government should be fair, just and even-handed, and that it should be for all of us.

I have to admit that after I retired Nancy's views began to influence me and make me think. For my part, I began to take more interest in the world, the people around me and the views of some of Nancy's friends, who tended to have left-wing sympathies. One evening in the late summer of 1980, Nancy told me that she was going to a special viewing of The War Game and asked if I would like to go with her. 'Why not?' I said. That evening would make more changes in me than I thought possible.

The film lasted for less than an hour. It told the story of another world war when presidents, generals, dictators and politicians used nuclear weapons to destroy their enemies and with them the world as we know it. It was utterly believable. I had taken too little notice of the destructive force of the two atomic bombs that had been dropped on Japan, hastening the end of the Second World War and possibly saving my life in Malaya. But there in front of me on the screen I could see what happens when an atomic missile explodes: the instant blindness of those who see the explosion, the resultant firestorm caused by the super-heated air and then the blast destroying everything that gets in its way. Following that there would be radiation sickness and severe psychological damage for those left alive amid a destroyed infrastructure. The film included a shot of British soldiers burning corpses, which made me feel physically sick.

I was shocked and shaking before the film even came to an end. It was much, much worse than anything I had experienced during the D-Day landings or at Nijmegen. It was clear that a nuclear war would be quite unlike anything that had gone before.
The film contained a quotation form Stephen Vincent Benet's poem Song for Three Soldiers:

'Oh where are you coming from, soldier, gaunt soldier
With weapons beyond any reach of my mind;
With weapons so deadly the world must grow older
And die in its tracks, if it does not turn kind?'

By the end of the film Nancy and I both knew we had do something. We joined the Campaign for Nuclear Disarmament (CND) on the spot. A week later I was appointed secretary of the newly formed Christchurch and New Forest CND Group. Would to God that in some small way we would be able to help prevent a nuclear war and the horrors it would bring. We had a world worth fighting for and I would do my best.

10

The Bravest Thing I Ever Did

Seeing *The War Game* and all it portrayed had a profound effect on me, which lasted for the rest of my life. It was so disturbing and so real. I could not get its horrors – and the sickening image of British soldiers burning bodies – out of my head. But something else had happened, too. Overnight I had been given a purpose in life, something I had lacked in recent years. I found myself excited and eager to help the growing Campaign for Nuclear Disarmament. Nancy was just as keen to help and we knew that together we could be a powerful team, working for the common good. As joint founder members of the Christchurch and New Forest CND, that's exactly what we tried to do.

But it was not just seeing the film that propelled me to join CND. By nature I had always been cautious, hardworking and sometimes slow to make up my mind, but for some years I had been worried about the spread of atomic weapons and what would happen if they got into the wrong hands. Admiral of the Fleet Louis Mountbatten had warned about their dangers and it was interesting that presidents Eisenhower and Carter, on leaving office and free to speak their minds, had said much the same thing.

The first atomic bombs, dropped on Japan, had been greeted with rejoicing. Most regarded 'The Bomb' as instrumental in bringing the war with Japan to an end. And it wasn't until some years after the end of the war that people began to comprehend the scale of the atomic monster the Allies had created and which other countries were now copying.

In England, the Peace Movement, as it was first called, began to show itself as a real force when CND organised the Aldermaston March, held over the Easter Weekend of 1959. Supporters gathered together by the Atomic Weapons Establishment, near Aldermaston, and then marched to Trafalgar Square in London. The marchers made a great impression and were applauded along the route but, for the most part, they got little more than sympathy. They did, however, get support from the left wing of the Labour Party who, for a brief period, had sufficient votes to force their party to support the policy of unilateral disarmament. Hugh Gaitskell, the Labour leader, was horrified and had the decision reversed, though not without some difficulty.

CND's objectives were clear and comprehensive:

- The elimination of British nuclear weapons
- The cancellation of the British nuclear weapons system Trident and the deployment of nuclear weapons in Britain
- The global abolition of nuclear weapons
- The abolition of weapons of mass destruction and, in particular, those of a chemical and biological nature
- The establishment of a nuclear-free Europe and a Europe with no United States military bases
- The closure of the nuclear power industry

All in all, it was quite a wish list.

As I've already told you, back in the 50s and 60s I took little or no interest in politics and while I admired the Aldermaston marchers and what they stood for and CND's success in 1963 in helping to secure the World Nuclear Test Ban Treaty, I was too busy with my growing family and work to take any real notice of what was going on. And so it was not until 21 years after the first Aldermaston March that Nancy and I joined CND. I was determined to make up for lost time. There was much to do and following the deployment of Pershing missiles across Western Europe, there had been a resurgence of Cold War tensions between America and Russia. Britain, too, had added to the tension by replacing its Polaris armed submarines with Trident missiles.

In the early 1980s, CND membership grew rapidly and I attended a number of rallies, sometimes with Nancy and with other members of our family. At that time public support for unilateralism was very high, and in October 1981 CND's demonstration against the deployment of US Cruise missiles in Britain and elsewhere in Europe was one of the largest protests ever seen, with 300,000 people taking to the streets of London and a further three million mobilising across Europe. It was in London, at another CND rally, that Nancy, much to her delight, met Tony Benn, one of her heroes.

Before long, I had become Chairman of Christchurch and New Forest CND and, as an ex-services member, was asked to help with a number of different projects, the most memorable of which was to help a remarkable American, George Mizo, who had completed three tours of duty in Vietnam. I will tell you more about him later.

In September 1981, there was another, altogether surprising development in the peace movement when a Welsh group calling themselves 'Women for life on Earth' arrived at Greenham Common in Berkshire. They had marched from Cardiff to challenge the assembly of 96 Cruise missiles on the common. After a request to see the Base Commander was turned down, the women set up a peace camp just outside the RAF base. Nobody back then had any idea that the peace camp would last for 19 years and gain worldwide recognition.

A protest organised and led by women was highly unusual in those days and their camping outside the nuclear base for week after week in all kinds of weather was a triumph of energy, determination and organisation. This new movement was much admired and soon drew more supporters from across the land. At the same time, it attracted the world's press, focusing attention on atomic missiles, which were, and still are, a peril to mankind. The women who had set up the peace camp at Greenham Common soon decided that it should only involve women. This had an advantage in that they could use their identity as mothers to legitimise their protest against nuclear weapons in the name of their children and future generations. The numbers varied but even in the harshest of weather, and despite the bullying and sometimes unpleasant attention of a number of the police and camp guards, the women stood firm and maintained their vigil. They were proactive, too. On New Year's Eve 1982, 44 women climbed over the perimeter fence. All were arrested and 36 sent to prison. Then, in December 1983, 50,000 women circled the base to protest against a delivery of Cruise missiles, which had arrived three weeks earlier.

Nancy started to visit Greenham Common but she could not do this on a regular basis because in the early 1980s she was still very busy with her costume business. Sometimes I would take her in my car and on other occasions she would go with friends. On my visits I could not help but be impressed by the way the women had organised themselves but I took a real dislike to some of the guards and police, who were more aggressive than they should have been.

For some reason that I did not fully understand, I found that after joining CND I began to think more about the war years than I had ever done before and with some trepidation I resolved to return to Sword Beach to attend the 40th Anniversary of the D-Day landings. I wanted to warn my fellow veterans about the perils of a nuclear war. Would they listen to me? Probably not, but I would try.

I caught the ferry to Le Havre, becoming more nervous by the day. I had taken my bicycle, of which I was very fond but now, like its owner, it was past retirement. Still, it had three rather smart Sturmey Archer gears and a nice big basket up front where I could store all my kit. Le Havre to Ouistreham is less than 20 miles, an easy cycle ride over two days, so I stopped at Deauville for the first night. The town looked in good order – smart, cosmopolitan, prosperous and advertising a top-class race meeting for the Sunday. I remembered one of the very few times I had been racing and that was at Doncaster, where Nancy and I had a good win, a really good win. Perhaps I would stop in Deauville on my way home and chance my arm.

The following day I got up early; I had a plan. I would take my bicycle over the Bailey bridge – now called London Bridge – which the Royal Engineers had built over the River Orne on D-Day plus one. Then I would have a coffee and some breakfast in the Pegasus Café, which was next to the bridge over the canal. I wondered whether I would be better off having a few beers for Dutch courage.

When I finally reached the beach, I felt a sort of nostalgia for my time in the military but I still felt it had been right for me to leave my medals at home. Nancy had made me a casual, battledress-style suit especially for the occasion and I carried a home-made placard which read:

CND – HELP SAVE THE WORLD I FOUGHT FOR

But everybody else on that beach had done exactly the same thing as me in 1944 – what would they think of my boast? I was still very nervous, maybe the best thing to do was to get on my bike and go home, but I stood there with my hands shaking throughout the ceremonies. Then it was all over and, to my amazement, I was surrounded by friends.

'Is this your first visit?' 'Very nice to see you.' 'I reckon your boys saved my life.' 'CND is the only hope for us,' said a Royal Naval officer in uniform, who squeezed my shoulder. 'Your boys got me off the beach and gave me a shower. I stank something awful.' Suddenly, remarkably, all was well. I had been accepted and a surprising number of those I spoke to were prepared to talk about what the nuclear age might bring. 'No effing good' was the popular verdict – and how right they were. And later in the day a high-ranking Army officer took me to one side and whispered over an impressive row of medals: 'You are absolutely right you know.'

After the ceremonies, which I found very moving, I had a marvellous time, with everybody being so very friendly. We had some beers, an excellent meal with Calvados and then we all joined in with a sing-song, which included many of the numbers I loved. I remembered the piano I had rescued from the bunker. I hoped that it was still being played. I had taken a quick look at the bunker; it was still there, but it was little more than a shabby concrete wall.

Heading for home, I knew that some day I would return to Ouistreham and, hopefully, bring some of my family. It was with this thought in mind that I left my name with a local immobilier (estate agent). It was more than a coincidence that later I would meet the owner of the business, one Fabrice Corbin. Neither of us knew it but we had something in common – an interest in the Grand Bunker.

It took me three days before I had pedalled myself back to Le Havre. The weather was good and I much enjoyed exploring the French countryside. Losing my sense of direction on narrow roads overhung with trees, I had to use my compass on several occasions. It was a good job I had brought it with me but you will know by now that I am that kind of man. Most of the fields were as small as I remembered them – no wonder the Allied advance was held up for such a long time in countryside much easier to defend than attack. Normandy was exceptional, but nothing like as grand as the Pennines of my youth.

11

Vietnam And The Remarkable George Mizo

As Chairman of the Christchurch and New Forest CND and as an ex-services member, I was asked to help with a number of different projects. Often I had to travel to London and it was there that Nancy and I met an American, George Mizo, who had completed three tours of duty in Vietnam.

The Vietnam conflict never, thank God, became an atomic war, but the destruction inflicted by American bombing and the use of chemical weapons defoliated the forests, depopulated great swathes of the country and caused great suffering. There were more dead than could be counted. Fortunately, the British Prime Minister, Harold Wilson, had resisted the pressure to support the war. It could have been that the vociferous activities of CND had helped him to make up his mind.

Nancy and I liked George Mizo from the moment we met him, and his was not the kind of name we would easily forget. We listened to his story. He told us what a wonderful country Vietnam was and about the war, which had appalled him and many of his fellow soldiers:

'Of course,' he told us, 'when Saigon was taken in 1975 and the war came to a messy finish, with America withdrawing its troops and bombers, most servicemen just wanted to get home and forget about the whole bloody affair. So did I, but I found that I couldn't do that. The things I had seen and done preyed on my mind.'

Angry and depressed, George then spent three years of his life demonstrating, and often sleeping, on the steps of the Capitol in Washington, telling anyone who would listen what had really happened in Vietnam and Cambodia – not just the physical destruction but the damage inflicted on the hearts and minds of its people.

'For the most part,' he continued, 'I was left alone by the authorities. I am sure that most Americans knew in their hearts that the war had been a terrible mistake.'

But George had wanted to do more than just tell his story: he wanted to try to make amends of some sort, and so it was that he had arrived in London, bringing with him money that he wanted to donate to a team of English doctors and their assistants working in Vietnam and Cambodia.

'Bob,' he said, 'they are a wonderful bunch of people and I would like to expand on what they are doing. Would you fly out and take them the money on my behalf?'
'Who exactly are they?' I asked.

'They are the Medical and Scientific Aid to Vietnam and Cambodia – quite a mouthful – but they are doing great work. I would go myself but almost certainly I would not be allowed into Vietnam and, if I were, the money would be confiscated.'
'Are you sure?' I asked.

'Certain,' George replied. 'After the way we Americans treated their beautiful country. But you are a Britisher who didn't take sides, so please take my contribution and deliver it to my friends. I would be so very grateful.'

I was very reluctant to accept the commission, though not exactly sure why, but George was not well and was in such a low state after his war-time experiences that I felt I had to do what he asked. So just three weeks later, I found myself on a plane bound for the Far East. The last time I had been to that part of the world was in 1945, when the journey had taken over two weeks by ship. But this time in just two short days I was in Ho Chi Minh City, being greeted by the friendliest of people. As far as I could tell, the Vietnamese bore little or no grudge against the Americans but maybe I was deceived by their unfailing good manners.

Much of the Vietnamese countryside was so very beautiful that it took my breath away. I saw the mighty Mekong River and then, travelling north by train, the paddy fields and green forests, which covered much of the country. Damage from the war was still visible but the multitude of women riding their bicycles would smile and never once did I feel any sense of danger. On arrival at the Medical and Scientific headquarters, not far from the northern capital of Hanoi, I met the British team of doctors and handed over a large envelope containing Mizo's extraordinary collection of dollar bills, cheques and money drafts. All was agreed with little fuss or bother, and with that my job was done. But I was somewhat surprised that the American dollar was the preferred currency so soon after the war.

Before I returned to the airport I was shown round several refugee camps, makeshift hospitals, orphanages and care centres, where the medical aid team would carry out operations and help patients in any way they could. There was even laughter in the temporary hospitals and I was only sorry that I could not understand a word of what was going on.

When I finally got back to Ho Chi Minh City I had to wait a day before my flight back to England, so I decided to take a half-day tour of the city. I wanted to take a bicycle but I was waved away: 'You are too heavy, mate!' said a shopkeeper in perfect English. But the tour of the city was very interesting and I was even shown the network of underground tunnels which the Viet Cong used to infiltrate their troops into the very centre of the city that was once Saigon.

Oddly, my trip to Vietnam was a real tonic for me personally – it left me with the strong feeling that there was still hope for the world. It was good, too, for me to be able to tell George Mizo that our mission had been successful and about the wonderful work that was being done by his friends and colleagues. As I told George about the warmth of the ordinary people I had met and how kind and friendly they had been, he nearly wept,

'That's how they are,' he said, 'and we dropped bombs on them.'

Nancy and I became firm friends with George. He was a lovely man and slowly but surely he seemed to be recovering his spirits and his health. Bit by bit we learned a little more about his life:

George was born in 1945. At the age of 14, when his father had become ill but had no health insurance, George had to leave school and go to work. Three years later, he joined the American Army as a soldier, and by dint of hard work and enthusiasm he became their youngest sergeant. He had twice been stationed in Vietnam and volunteered to return when war broke out, becoming what was known as a 'fighting sergeant' in the forefront of an increasingly brutal conflict. As Sergeant George, he had to accept responsibility for what was done in his sector: the murder of innocent villagers, the destruction of their homes with napalm, and many other atrocities. And all the while (though not, of course, George's responsibility) American bombers rained death and destruction from above on so many innocent people.

Wounded three times, George was invalided back to America but when he recovered he was ordered to return to Vietnam. He refused to go on conscientious grounds. Fair enough, you might have thought, but he was sent to prison for two years for disobeying orders. As it happened, the whole of George Mizo's troop was lost in the fighting, while George's own life was to be shortened by chemical poisoning from the defoliant with the sinister name of Agent Orange.

Over the next few years, Nancy and I continued to meet George and were delighted when, in 1992, he founded the Vietnam Friendship Village, which included as partners the team of doctors and helpers working for Medical and Scientific. George became chairman and was soon allowed back into Vietnam. The village proved to be a great success, winning international acclaim, much of it due to George's hard work and personality. At a CND meeting in France in 1991, where we were both delegates, I witnessed the force of that personality and George's remarkable ability to make friends with people of many different nationalities while simultaneously getting things done. On a personal note, George found contentment with a lovely German woman who became his wife,and a baby only added to their joy.

George Mizo died in 2002 at the age of 56. He had lived for longer than he or anybody else had expected but in the end Agent Orange had done him too much damage. I like to think, though, that George's wife, their child and the great and enduring success of the Vietnam Friendship Village brought him some peace and happiness.

12

From Greenham To Holloway

If anybody had told me that Nancy would be sent to prison, and to Holloway of all places – one of the toughest jails in England – I would never have believed them. But that's exactly what happened and, despite my best endeavours, there was nothing I could do to keep her out. She was determined to do her bit for CND and once Nancy had decided what she wanted to do she had nerves of steel. Some members of the family were cross and regarded her incarceration as shameful. That was nonsense, of course, but could I understand their concern. I have no doubt that most of my friends and family blamed me more than Nancy but, to be frank, that didn't worry me – people could think what they damn well liked. I have to admit, though, that the time when she was arrested was one of the rare occasions when I was glad my father was not around. He would have made an almighty fuss, shouting and swearing, but in the end he would have given Nancy a kiss and told her gently that she was a silly girl. Maybe I should have done the same.

As I've already told you, in 1980, when we both joined CND with high hopes that we could put the world to rights, Nancy was very busy with her costume business and I know she felt guilty that she was not doing enough for the women on Greenham Common who she so admired. Then in 1983 Christchurch Council decided it wanted us to return the short lease we had taken on the property we had converted for Nancy's costume gallery. And so it was that we closed the gallery and Nancy gave away her collection to those who needed a helping hand and to a host of good causes which she wanted to help. All of us – family, friends and helpers – thought we would miss the business, which had become part of our lives, but the business had a momentum all of its own and in a strange way carried on regardless. Nancy continued to help anybody who wanted a costume. On one occasion an actor came to the house because he was sure that Nancy would make him look the part he was to play the following week. 'I just don't like what I have been given,' he told her. In a few short years Nancy had become very well known in Christchurch, both for her personality and her skills, and so, business or no business, the telephone kept ringing. And at home little had changed – our new house was cluttered with costumes. That never bothered me.

Once the business was closed – at least officially – Nancy was able to spend more time at Greenham Common and I, while always putting the welfare of our family first, did my best to support her. The CND movement became a very important part of our lives but still I like to think that it didn't change us too much. We still loved a party, seeing friends, going to the theatre or cinema, but best of all we enjoyed a good dinner with beer, wine and talking – and sometimes singing – with those we loved.

The Greenham Common peace camp is now a well-known part of our recent history and you might think that the Greenham women had an interesting and exciting time. Of course, there were moments of drama, such as when part of the perimeter fence was torn down and a crowd of protesters managed, for a few hours, to close one of the main gates. But in truth the day-to-day reality was very different: there was more drudgery than excitement, long nights, lack of sleep, rain, cold, even snow, poor food and a complete lack of privacy and comfort. And, often as not and almost always early in the morning, the police and security guards would make things as difficult as they could for those trying to get some rest. But, despite everything, the protesters were proud of what they were doing and when another day was done there was more laughter than tears.

Nancy liked her independence but I often drove her to the Common in my elderly car, a Datsun. It was an easy journey from Christchurch to Greenham, about an hour's drive travelling due north. Over the months, I began to know a few of the women on Blue Gate, which was Nancy's station, but I never stayed too long – it was made very clear that the Greenham women were in charge and I respected that. But bit-by-bit Nancy told me of the night-time difficulties, when council bailiffs would come along in the early hours and confiscate dry firewood, spare clothing, food and water. It was the women who were posted at Blue Gate who were particularly vulnerable as it was the first and easiest access to the Greenham Common Aerodrome. How could I help? It was a challenge that the budding inventor within me relished and in a few days I had built a secure trolley in the shape of a large trunk connected to two strong bicycle wheels, which was easy to push, even when loaded. I purloined a large piece of blue plastic to keep the damp and wet off.

The trolley was a great success. I still have the letter of thanks from the women of Blue Gate:

Thank you so much Nancy and Bobo.

Yes it has been a long time but we were waiting for these photos to be printed to send you.

We all were most overjoyed with the trolley (named Marja) and it has become an indispensible part of Blue Gate.

Many a thing has been kept dry and safe from the bailiffs thanks to your efforts, and there have been several evictions of which I would hate to imagine what would have happened without Marja. She is wonderfully easy to move about.

Thanks again – the girls of Blue Gate

Despite the letter and all that Nancy was doing for her companions on Blue Gate, she still felt guilty and thought she had not done enough for the cause.

'We have had such an easy life compared with those women out on the Common night after night,' she told me, and, being Nancy, she decided that she would do something more to help. She found a small hacksaw in our garage and took it with her when she next joined the protesters on Blue Gate. Then, in full view of the police, she began to saw at the perimeter fence, not that her small saw would make any impression on the fence, which was a massive construction. A policeman of a kindly nature asked Nancy to stop sawing. She wouldn't, of course, and eventually he was forced to charge her with a breach of the peace. He told her if she paid a fine of £25 no further action would be taken, but if she did not pay she would be sent to prison and that would be unpleasant.

I gave Nancy £25 and insisted that she kept it with her at all times – the last thing I wanted was for her to be jailed but, of course, that was exactly what Nancy had in mind – she thought it would be the best way that she could help the peace movement. Nothing happened for some days, but when finally one morning she was asked to pay the fine and refused she was put in a police van and driven straight to Holloway to serve a two-week sentence.

I was upset and very worried – Holloway had a grim reputation. It was a massive prison, built in Victorian times and notorious for being the last place in England where a female prisoner – Ruth Ellis – was hanged. However, while Nancy found the whole process of being a prisoner degrading, she was in no way treated badly and, much to her surprise, was sent home at the end of just one week, despite her sentence being for two. The thing that most upset Nancy during her time in Holloway was hearing a woman crying in her dormitory because her sister would not visit her. 'It's because I am a jailbird,' she had sobbed. Back home, Nancy was rather depressed about the whole business but was much cheered when a man she hardly knew knocked on the door.

'I would like to shake you by the hand,' he said. 'It is a fine thing to go to prison on a matter of conscience.'

The Greenham Common protest continued for the better part of 20 years and only ended after all the nuclear missiles had been removed from the site – not everything that Nancy, her friends and CND had hoped for, but certainly better than nothing.

13

To Russia With Peace

Towards the end of the 1980s, CND had begun to recognise that ex-servicemen and women would be among the best possible people to help it achieve its aims. Those who had served in the armed forces would have experienced the realities of conventional warfare – its suffering, terror and hardship – and they, perhaps more than most, would be able to comprehend that, in comparison, a nuclear war would be unspeakably awful and on a scale that humankind would not be able to control.

By the early 1990s, I had been a member of CND for ten years and I still hoped with all my heart that we might succeed and rid the world of nuclear weapons once and for all. Being retired and reasonably fit, I had the time to assist with a number of projects. In April 1991, if for no other reason than it was my turn, I found myself elected Chairman of the CND Ex-Services Committee. Then, to our complete astonishment, Nancy and I were given just two weeks' notice to attend an important event in Russia. We were to be the guests of the Russian Veterans of War in Moscow on May 7,1991, and while in Moscow we would be expected to attend the Commemoration of the 50th Anniversary of the Start of The Great Patriotic War of The Soviet People (announcements of this kind in Russia tend to be long-winded). We were to fly by Aeroflot, which gave me some concern, as in those days the Russian carrier had a reputation for bangs and crashes.

The question of what we should take and what we should wear exercised our minds. Nancy, as usual, was quick off the mark and found we had room in our baggage allowance for some food and small treats for children, and so it was that we ended up taking with us a very large box of apples, which, Nancy had been told, would be much appreciated. Would it snow? Well of course it didn't – the snow is gone before May, even in Moscow. And Aeroflot, despite my concern, was on its best behaviour transporting us in comfort to Russia and landing us safely at Moscow Airport.

On arrival, we were at once whisked away by a charming professor of English, Gregory Veikhman, who, with a personal interpreter, took us to the VIP lounge, outlined our programme and then on to the 4,000 bed Hotel Rossiya, large beyond belief, with the longest corridors I had ever seen. But there was compensation – from our bedroom window we had a glorious view of a magnificent church and its dome just a few feet below.

Our first official engagement was a ceremony at the Tomb of the Unknown Warrior, where I laid a floral tribute of peonies and a dove of peace. And then, hardly stopping to draw breath, we were taken to the Bolshoi Theatre. We were rather surprised that our passports were checked and then checked again at the entrance. The reason soon became apparent when, in the wonderful and glittering surroundings of that great theatre, President Gorbachev made a speech. He spoke for well over an hour about the evils of Stalin and then announced the ending of military conscription. Everyone seemed very happy, except perhaps for the military chiefs sitting in the audience who were going to have fewer troops to boss. But it was indeed a remarkable announcement, made in front of a large gathering of the world's press, and it certainly gave us good cheer.

So why were the world's press sitting there in the Bolshoi that night along with Nancy and me? Well, although we didn't really know it then, our visit was being made at one of the most critical times in post-war history. The nuclear arms race between Russia and America had gone on for too long, and for all practical purposes the Soviet Union was bankrupt and simply could not match the pace with which America was producing missiles, each deadlier than the last. Gorbachev knew the score and using his remarkable skills had reached an uneasy compromise with President Reagan and the Western powers. If Russia had been led by a lesser man there could well have been a nuclear strike from either side. But that evening Nancy and I were not thinking too much about a nuclear war. We were just two ordinary people from Christchurch, England, sitting waiting for President Gorbachev to finish so we could listen to some music and see some dancing.

Our second day in Russia was very different. We were to watch the annual May Day Parade of the Russian armed services which, bankrupt or not, was still one of the largest and most powerful armies in the world. The theme of the massive parade we were to witness was the years 1945 to 1990. It took us a long time to find our seats before we were finally ushered into the Foreign Veterans stand overlooking the Kremlin Wall, with Lenin's Tomb on our right. Troops marched past in blocks of 100, their drill immaculate. There were tributes to those who had helped Russia in her hour of need – a Free French air squadron and British sailors who had served on the Russian convoys. At the end of the parade, nuclear missiles lumbered past on great trucks. Nancy closed her eyes.

Later that evening, walking along the banks of the Moskva River, we met a man who told us he was the political correspondent for Pravda. I had no reason to disbelieve him but it seemed curious that we should meet such a person on that particular day. But he was very pleasant and before parting told us that a group of young men wearing fatigues on the other side of the road were veterans, too, mostly young soldiers from the Russian–Afghan War. 'Some of them had a very bad time,' he said.

The next day was devoted to a conference attended by representatives of the 56 war veteran associations, who had gathered together in Moscow. The conference venue was a mighty hall on top of a hill but, for the moment, I can't remember its name. I was due to speak that afternoon. Was I nervous? Of course, but I had prepared my speech and was confident that I would get a fair hearing.

A Marshal of the Soviet Union opened the conference. He was conciliatory and forward-looking and gave the kind of speech that would not have been heard in Russia until very recently. All the speeches were simultaneously translated into four languages, one of which was English, so we could understand what was going on. The speeches, as you might imagine, were an odd mixture, some expressing very personal views on particular problems, but there was much concern about the prospect of a united Germany and no wonder – few of us at the conference were in a mood to forgive or forget what the Germans had done in the Second World War. My suggestion that an international association for all peace-orientated veterans be formed was well received and got some applause.

That evening, Professor Veikhman and his wife gave us a delicious meal at their house and we met their two daughters, one of whom taught English at a university. The other daughter was a singer and she kindly gave us one of her records. As it happened, the professor's house was near a cemetery where many of Russia's famous sons are buried. A knowledgeable guide (the Professor's wife) made our walk among those tombs an interesting history lesson.

Back in our room at the hotel we still had our great box of apples and we were both worried that they might go off if we kept them any longer. We could certainly smell them, particularly when we woke up in the morning. It was now the fourth day of our stay and I had yet another meeting to attend but Nancy, with an hour or two to spare, solved the problem. She took up her box of apples, which was so heavy she could hardly carry it, together with the gifts she had brought for young children, and hailed a taxi. Nancy struck lucky with her driver and within a very short time she was handing over apples and gifts to an appreciative English-speaking doctor in the paediatric department of a local hospital.

Our crowded five days culminated in a formal reception. Language was a problem but we all smiled at each other and already, in just a few days, we were making friends. We all enjoyed a magnificent firework display from the six points of the city and as a finale were given splendid seats for the Moscow State Circus. Then it was back to the airport and another trouble-free and punctual flight on Aeroflot to Heathrow.

Some time after our visit, Professor Veikhman and a lawyer from Georgia arrived in London. They came as members of the Anglo-Soviet Friendship Holiday Scheme. Our youngest son, Martin, who was by then a doctor, met the two of them at the airport and so it was that that remarkable man started a friendship with the next generation. Martin was soon to visit Russia on an exchange visit and was able to see part of that extraordinary country for himself.

My next trip was to America to promote my suggestion for an international association of peace-oriented veterans. Our first formal act was to issue a warning communiqué on the Gulf Crisis. Would to God that more people had taken notice of what we had to say.

14

To France And New Zealand

By 1991, almost without my noticing, I had become a bit of a world traveller. And to think that my very first venture away from Britain had been to land on that bloody Sword Beach and on D-Day. I sometimes wonder whether I would ever have bothered to travel abroad were it not for the war. I have always been at my happiest exploring the Lake District or walking the Pennines. But in my seventies I found, much to my surprise, that I was clocking up the air miles.

I wondered why I had been so reluctant, even afraid, to fly to Vietnam to help George Mizo. He and his fellow soldiers had wanted to repair some of the terrible damage America had inflicted on Vietnam and Cambodia, so why my hesitation? Perhaps I had been afraid of seeing another battlefield. It had taken me the better part of 40 years to accept what I had seen on the beaches and the battlefields near Caen. And then there had been the bridge at Nijmegan, Holland, where I had lost good friends and where, for months on end, we had been under fire from the enemy just a few miles upriver in Germany. But, in a strange way, the visit to Vietnam had done me good. I returned home less gloomy about the future. It was shocking, of course, that the American military, when it realised it was losing the war, had used chemical weapons. But in the end, and despite America's humiliating defeat, it had not resorted to the use of nuclear weapons. Perhaps the world had learned just a little after all. It was the same when I travelled to Russia and Gorbachev's remarkable speech at the Bolshoi gave us hope. While Gorbachev did not support the kind of disarmament we in CND advocated, that speech had been a turning point – conscription had been abolished and Russia's armed services reduced. The speech may have cost him his job, but a counter-revolution failed.

Anyway, in October 1991, as leader of the British CND Ex-Services team, I led our delegates to a three-day congress in Nantes, France. I found it very heartening to be in a hall with more than 500 French ex-servicemen who fervently shared our desire for world peace. I felt that our French colleagues were much better at telling their government what it should do than we were at telling ours. We were just so deferential.

'We should follow the French example,' I said to my colleagues. 'They never allowed nuclear weapons in their country.'

It was my privilege to address the congress on Sunday. I used a quotation from Martin Luther King as the starting point for my speech: 'We must learn to live together as brothers or perish together as fools.'

The quotation was picked up by several of the following speakers, including the President. I was delighted, and I had made my speech in French, so it was a comfort to know that at least some of those in the audience knew what I was talking about.
Among the delegates was my friend George Mizo, for whom a couple of years earlier I had flown to Vietnam. I was delighted to learn that his charity was doing well and earning the trust of the Vietnamese and Cambodian people. And George looked relaxed and cheerful – much better than the last time I last saw him. I suspected his new wife and child might have something to do with it.

At the end of the congress there was a ceremony where George Mizo was kissed on both cheeks by our president, Georges Doussin, and was awarded a splendid French medal for his services to peace. There was much applause and, deeply touched, George told the audience that this was one medal 'I shall never give back'. He had returned all his service medals to the American government as a protest against the Vietnam War and American foreign policy. I was so impressed by the support Georges Doussin, an active and likeable man, was giving to George, helping him to realise his dream of the Vietnam Friendship Village.

Early in 1992, I took Nancy to New Zealand. I had some CND business to deal with and some friends to meet but we paid our own way, as our intention was to take a holiday and visit a part of the world that we had never seen. We had been inspired to visit that marvellous country by a chance meeting that Nancy had on Greenham Common a few years earlier.

New Zealanders had been very upset that the testing of atomic bombs had taken place in the South Pacific. There had also been a great deal of disquiet about the fact that American nuclear-powered battleships would enter Auckland harbour, despite being requested not to. Finally, things had come to a head and three young women working on their own, but with much help from local residents, managed to stop American warships from entering the harbour. Their plan had been simple, non-warlike, but very effective.

The three women, who were friends, visited all the residents whose homes fronted the harbour and persuaded a large number of them to drop banners in their front windows with suitable remarks such as No Nuclear Ships Allowed Here and some of a more earthy nature, such as Eff Off Yanks And Take Your Ships With You. The second stage of the plan was to ask all owners of small boats to sail them into Auckland harbour when the American nuclear ships were expected. The result was chaos. There was no room in the harbour, and the American commander, fearing that there might be a tragic accident, withdrew his ships. A week or two later, America imposed trade sanctions on New Zealand but there were other countries in the world that were pleased to buy the products America refused.

The trouble between America and New Zealand had been world news and Nancy, remarkably, met the three women involved. She had been sitting in a tent and flying a rainbow banner on Greenham Common when three women walked by.

'Hello!' said one to Nancy. 'We are from New Zealand.'
'I am so glad to meet you,' Nancy replied. 'I have been reading about how your women stopped American battleships entering Auckland.'

'That was us!' they said in chorus,
And so it was that a year or two later we made the long journey to New Zealand. The Caledonian girls – do you remember them? – looked after us and we had a safe and comfortable flight from Gatwick.

We first travelled to Christchurch, New Zealand. Coming from Christchurch, England, it seemed the right thing to do. A new park was being opened beside the town and we were impressed that a Maori citizen, one of New Zealand's indigenous population, performed the opening ceremony. Next to the park, we were shown some small university buildings. These had been given to the public as places where they could support good causes to the benefit of all. One of the buildings housed the Campaign for Nuclear Disarmament. It was called the Epicentre, short for 'Environment and Peace Information Centre'. What a good idea, we thought, and within a year we had opened a similar centre in Christchurch, England.

New Zealand exceeded all our expectations. It is a beautiful country and we so liked its people that we told our children that, if we hadn't had family in the UK, we might have thought of emigrating. And in New Zealand I could relax – I didn't have to tell New Zealanders why they should support CND, it seemed everyone I met was either a member or, at the very least, sympathetic to the cause, as was the country's government.

Following our stay in Christchurch, we had an invitation to visit an ex-services CND member in Wellington. His name was Chris King and he was also head of a local Arctic convoy group of veterans. Wellington Quay has a number of monuments to those who served in the Arctic convoys, performing their duties on those wild, cold and dangerous seas, with U–Boats waiting for their chance – the worst journey in the world.

Spending time with Chris was a joy – we became close friends on our first meeting and have remained so. Chris told us of a remarkable coincidence. Between long absences on convoy duty during the war, Chris had been sent on leave to Christchurch, England, and was given the use of two rooms in the upper part of a Bridge Street house for rest and recuperation. It was just yards from our own home. He told us how lovely it had been to see children playing on the grass, men fishing and swans gliding on the river. We asked him if he missed anything about England.

'Now and again when I want to post a letter, I can't seem to find a red pillar box. In New Zealand they are all white.'

All too soon our holiday was over but there had been time to explore some of New Zealand's marvellous countryside and enjoy meeting its kind and courteous people. Walking through that country's wide-open spaces, its hills and mountains, I had to confess, if only to myself, they were more than a match for the Pennines.

15

The Bunker Restored

I have told you about my lonely visit to Sword Beach on the 40th Anniversary of the D-Day landings, when, frightened and apprehensive and standing on the edge of things, I attended the annual commemoration service. Sick to my stomach, all I had wanted was to go home. I had been fearful about what my comrades might say when the service came to an end. And then, suddenly, I had been surrounded by friends wanting to talk to me, shake my hand and tell me how pleased they were to meet me. It was hard not to cry.

And then, on March 20, 1994, nearly ten years later, I was invited to meet Fabrice and Brigitte Corbin, who had bought the Grand Bunker and turned it into a museum, and a grand museum at that. Fabrice had been collecting military artefacts from Sword Beach and the surrounding area for many years. He had amassed quite a collection of old weapons and other bits and pieces and had even helped to recover a sunken 'Priest' armoured vehicle. He had learned a lot about D-Day and had become quite an expert on the subject. When the opportunity to rent 'Le Grand Bunker' came up in the late 1980s, Fabrice and his wife, Brigitte, set about clearing out many years of debris. They then set up 'Le Grand Bunker – Museum of the Atlantic Wall', the finest restoration of a German bunker on the Normandy Wall.

My meeting with the Corbins went well. I knew from the very start we would become good friends. I was introduced to them by Nicholas Dumont. Nicholas was an interesting man, the assistant curator of the Airborne Museum at Bénouville, who had previously worked at the Arromanches D-Day Museum, and his excellent English was a great help during my visit.

When I saw the bunker restored I could scarcely believe that it was the same structure I had seen on my last visit – then it had been nothing more than a dirty, decaying hulk set in a rubbish dump – and I marvelled as Fabrice and Brigitte took me round their museum. I was delighted with their skill and attention to detail. Somehow they had managed to bring the place to life, so much so that I half expected to meet the German officer who had called out to me in the night almost 50 years earlier: 'Come upstairs, Johnny, it's all right!' The bloody cheek of it! Yes, the Corbins had done a marvellous job. It can't have easy with tons of rubbish to remove and those great thick walls.

After many Gallic hugs and kisses, I said goodbye to the Corbins, promising them that I would be back in Ouistreham for the D-Day celebrations in five weeks' time.
'And my daughter and her husband, they're coming, too,' I told them.
'Then you must all come to our party,' Brigitte had replied.

More laughter, goodbyes and excitement. Indeed, there was already excitement in the air in Ouistreham, with flowers being planted along the quayside where the Royal Yacht Britannia was to be moored before she made her way nine miles up the canal to Caen, a town which had been extensively rebuilt after its destruction in 1944 in one the bloodiest battles that the British Army had ever fought. I, too, was excited. It seemed that the 50th anniversary was, as they say in the North Country, going to be a right good do.

My daughter, Christine, and her husband, Ralph, were on a cycling tour of Normandy, taking in Bayeux and Arromanches, and had agreed to meet me off the overnight ferry the day before the anniversary. As arranged, they were waiting for me at 0700 hours. Already the town was busy but I knew where we could find some breakfast – it would be my treat – and how good it was to relax with a decent cup of coffee. Why is French coffee so much better than ours? Christine and Ralph told me about their adventures and the wonders of Bayeux. I think we may have spent too much of our time at the bunker during our stay but I was anxious to give the Corbins as much help as possible. As an engineer, I had a sense of just how expensive the restoration must have been. But, of course, if I was honest, there was another reason: Fabrice's wine and beer were far too good to miss.

But I did find time to take Christine and Ralph to see the Bailey bridges of which I was so very proud. I told them all about the bridges and how the Bailey bridge across the river Orme had been built in three hours on D-Day plus one. After some little time, the two of them moved away, perhaps hoping for another cup of coffee at the Pegasus Café and giving me a hint that they had seen enough of my bridge building. As I moved away, a young man with very long hair (the kind of thing I notice) who had overheard our conversation smiled and said
'All that in three hours, some going Mister!'

'Yes!' I told him, but I had to do a bit of explaining.

Christine, Ralph and I were astonished by the number of visitors in the town. The arrival of Britannia was greeted with cheers. Britannia herself looked marvellous, she sparkled in the occasional sunlight and would certainly be the star of the show when she moored in the centre of Caen. Hundreds of small yachts and motor launches had made their way to Ouistreham together with Britannia. It was quite a sight but a hazardous journey for the many small craft to make, some of them less than 25ft. Rather them than me, I thought. I have never been able to forget feeling as sick as I did on that miserable tank landing craft wallowing in the swell off Sword Beach.

The evening before the official celebrations the three of us went to Brigitte's party in the bunker. I enjoyed myself and it was good to meet so many nice people. I found it humbling that so many should ask for my autograph. I had to keep explaining that the four of us, including Big Jim, had not been particularly brave; we were just doing what we had been told to do. As for the Germans viewing the great Allied armada from their tower, they must have known that their war was lost.

'All they wanted to do was surrender,' I told the partygoers. 'My greatest difficulty was finding the prisoners of war compound in the dark.'

It was an altogether memorable and fun evening, with singing, which I have always loved, and – Fabrice and Brigitte being very generous hosts – some very good food. At about midnight, while we were still enjoying our cheese, we were interrupted by a knocking on one of the high windows of the bunker. Fabrice opened the door and there outside were three Royal Marines. They told us that they had tried to take the bunker on D-Day but had been quite unable to blow down the door with their Sten guns.

'I am not surprised,' I told them, 'neither could we, and we almost ran out of explosives before we could do it.'

It was simply marvellous to meet those three Marines. So many of them had been killed in the initial landings but the Marines were brave and well-trained men who always seemed extraordinarily cheerful. After exchanging our stories, it was time for another sing-song and then for bed

The following morning there were the usual services for us veterans. I found myself standing close to Lord Lovat's piper, Bill Millin, the same piper who had been heard on D-Day by the British Airborne troops defending Pegasus Bridge against a superior German force. What marvellous news it must have been to learn that help was on the way. I was much moved by the commemoration service, as were Christine and Ralph.

After lunch the three of us cycled in drizzling rain along the coastal path to Lion-sur-Mer, where the new Royal Engineers Cemetery was to be dedicated. Then, without warning, I was overcome with sorrow remembering comrades and friends whom I had loved and I broke down in tears. Goodness knows what Christine must have thought but I didn't care. Perhaps part of the problem was that I had been drinking a bit too much that day. The three of us had one more day together and then we went home, with our thoughts and our memories, by the morning ferry.

16

Retirement? Not If I Could Help It

As I grew older, I noticed that a long walk took me a little longer than it would have done in the past and that it was sensible, sometimes, to sit down and get a little more air into my lungs. And then there was my memory: it had always been very good and still was but sometimes without warning I would forget the name of someone I had just met. I was, as I once heard in a song, 'shorter in wind, as in memory long'.

Nevertheless, Nancy and I kept busy and happy, and when we returned from our wonderful trip to New Zealand in 1993 we had exciting plans for the future. We were determined that Christchurch, England, should have an Epicentre run on exactly the same lines as the one we had seen in Christchurch, New Zealand. Easier said than done perhaps, as Christchurch Borough Council tended to be conservative when it came to new ideas. But, as it happened, there was a derelict prefabricated building, which was no use to anybody, in the park close to where we lived. So we got together with a few friends and told the council that we would renovate the building at no cost. That did the trick and within a few weeks the Christchurch Environmental and Peace Information Centre – the Epicentre, as we called it – was up and running. It was soon to play an important part in our local community life, supporting many good causes including the University of the Third Age. Like it or not, Nancy and I were both eligible and before long we were going to their lectures.

I much enjoyed my work for the Epicentre and had soon collected a substantial library of leaflets and literature on organisations we thought worthy of support. I marvelled at the number of groups that were doing their best to help our troubled world: Greenpeace, Oxfam, The Woodland Trust, Friends of The Earth, Liberty, the UN Association and the RSPB to name but a few and, of course, CND, which was always at the front of our displays. The Epicentre kept us busy and through its activities we both met many interesting people, some whom we would bring home for a coffee or a beer. Nancy had not lost her love of entertaining.

Nancy and I also helped in the promotion of local events and I laughed when I came home one day to find an old press cutting announcing a medieval fayre on the kitchen table:

LOCAL MEDIEVAL FAYRE

Christchurch Borough Council's Leisure Officer Sue Harman Smith is organising the above event. She envisages a touch of the 16th century, with people in costume selling crafts, homemade goods, etc. The background could be a bale or two of straw or a wattle fence, so it sounds fun.

'I've got the costumes if you have got the goods!' Nancy had written at the bottom of the page.

Nancy still loved her extraordinary costume business, but gradually, almost without our noticing, age was catching up with both of us, slowing us down just when we wanted to find more time for our children and grandchildren. The Epicentre, CND and the costume business were getting too much. In the end it was Nancy who made the decision: 'Make us some Nazi uniforms!' a group of hooligans coming out of a pub yelled at her one day. Nancy told them in no uncertain terms what she thought of them but decided then and there to close her costume business. But, of course, she kept her hand in for friends and special customers, and our house at Wickfield Avenue remained packed with special costumes of every shape and size.

One of the things that did surprise me in my later years was how much I looked forward to the D-Day celebrations in Ouistreham when, in the immediate post-war years, nothing would have persuaded me to go anywhere near the place. But now I valued Fabrice and Brigitte's friendship and would happily join them for hours on end in their brilliantly restored bunker. And then there were my fellow veterans, who had landed on that beach all those years ago. We were all friends now, past differences forgiven or forgotten. As for myself, there is nothing quite like a beer in the French sunshine. I should have like to have shared a drink with one of the 50 or so German soldiers I had captured. Sadly, Jonathan and Christine, despite their best endeavours, could find no trace – the German records had been destroyed. On June 6 every year, the anniversary of D-Day, I returned to Normandy, sometimes more often.

At home things went on in much the same way. I would still dress myself up to be the town crier and would regularly ride my bicycle to the Burley Youth Centre, where I acted as an unofficial planner and self-appointed odd job man, undertaking cleaning, mending and building repairs. I was pretty good at those kind of things. And up to the age of 80, I was still able to do some walking with my family, but no longer as their undisputed leader, as I had been in the past. From 80 onwards, it seemed that I was beginning to fall apart: a new hip that didn't work properly (I had enthusiastically attempted to ride my bicycle too soon after the operation) and a touch of cancer that didn't want to go away.

But even then there were compensations, and having the time to get to know friends really well was one of them. You will remember my telling you about Professor Gregory Veikhman, whom Nancy and I had met in Russia. A great admirer of Britain, he came to live in Christchurch for several months every year. He told me about the time he was involved, as a Russian soldier, at the siege of Stalingrad and also something about the history of his extraordinary and enigmatic country. He believed that it was the Russian convoys orchestrated by Britain that had saved his life. Starving and freezing during the siege, with only a threadbare uniform, he had been given a new uniform – warm comfortable and well made – with a note: From the people of Britain. I was lucky in other ways. I still had enough skill in my hands to make homemade presents for my grandchildren, a hobby which I always enjoyed, and I was still able to write a stiff letter to the council if I thought it was making a mistake on a planning matter. Added to that, Nancy and I had many happy memories of our adventures, particularly when they had involved our children. Joining our youngest son, Martin, in Bali, Indonesia, was one such occasion. He had just become a doctor and we had adjoining cabins on the beach. Nancy told us that she wanted to fly on a parachute she had seen being towed by a speedboat – not my kind of thing at all, but Nancy had nerves of steel when she wanted to do something. Waking up the next morning, she was nowhere to be seen. I went to the beach, looked up and there was Nancy flying very high! There was a bit of trouble with her harness but, to my relief, she landed safely. We had a great week's holiday with Martin in a beautiful country, with its kind and gentle people.

It was early in November 2002 that Nancy and I heard the terrible news that our eldest son, Robert, had died. It was difficult to believe that such a good man and caring doctor should be taken from us. His funeral took place in the Cathedral Church of St Peter in Exeter. The large congregation and the singing was of some comfort and, casting my walking sticks aside, I managed to walk up the aisle to pay my last respects to a son whom I had so loved. My heart was full of bleak despair and anger, it was the worst day of my life, but I knew it was my duty to keep going and cherish Robert's family and this I did.

In 2002, I was selected by the Royal British Legion to recite the Kohima Epitaph during the Service of Remembrance in Bayeux Cathedral.

**"When you go home
Tell them of us and say
For your tomorrow
We gave our today"**

Finally, in June 2003, I was just fit enough to attend the D-Day celebrations. I had to spend more time than I liked in a wheelchair, but it was, as always, a privilege to be there.

17

And Finally …

Robert Orrell – Major, Royal Engineers, Chartered Civil Engineer, D-Day veteran and fervent peace campaigner was a great personality, singer, recycler, orator, leader and one of the most humorous people you could meet.

But most of all, he was our dad – 'Bob' to all those who had the pleasure to know him. Bob passed away less than a month after his visit to 'Le Grand Bunker' in Normandy for the 60th anniversary of D-Day in 2004 which, although very ill, he was determined to attend. (We, in the Orrell family, usually call it Bob's Bunker).

He had spent his last days after the commemorations at home before moving briefly to the nearby hospital in Christchurch. Although bedridden, he managed to stay alive for Nancy's 80th birthday on June 23 and died peacefully on the 30th, as if holding on till the time was right.

Shortly before his funeral, all the family got to see him one last time. He was organised to the last, even leaving instructions for his funeral (in his words):

Thoughts on a funeral
At the Chapel at the Woodland Burial Ground, Hinton, near Christchurch.

"A simple Humanist ceremony with CofE overtones if possible – like someone reading Psalm 23.

I don't want people – especially family – saying much about me. Everyone will have their own ideas and may as well stick to them. I'd like to think that someone could find the way to World Peace and Universal Love.

Thank them for coming.

Donations 50/50 Greenpeace / Oxfam rather than flowers.

Have a nice get together somewhere handy.

Love to all Bob

A cardboard coffin should do nicely."

Bob's last words were:

"…I just wanted to make sure that everyone's all right …"

He was a great family head and father, who understood that hard work was very important but, too, that rest and fun were also an integral part of life.

This apparent contradiction of hard work and fun, and the likelihood that his deep understanding of war was essential in making him such a great campaigner for peace, were very much part of Bob's make up.

Hard work and 'the endurance factor', as he used to call it, is part of what gets you through life. After all, he'd say: *'You can't enjoy sunshine without a rainy day or two.'*

To paraphrase Bob's words at our dear brother Robert's funeral:

"It looks like my children and grandchildren are adopting the same values of caring for people that we have. He was our son, of whom we were well proud!"

Well, Bob was our father, of whom we are all well proud.

We hope you have enjoyed the story of Bob's life and that The Regimental Piano has given you something to think about.

We started this book as a record but do think there's a message, too.

As for the piano – would that German officer or his troops have had any relief from the terrors of war when hearing it? How could he have known that his piano would have helped his opponents by being such a morale booster?

The Regimental Piano, last seen in Berlin in May 1945. We wonder where it is now.

The Orrell Family
December 2013

The beginning - Lieutenant Bob Orrell - 9ʰ June 1944

Conrad Lowen 2009

Major Bob Orrell - Final visit to the Grand Bunker 6th June 2004

Conrad Lawson 2009

15 & 16 THE BUNKER RESTORED:
RETIREMENT? NOT IF I COULD HELP IT

In 1984, I had returned to Normandy to campaign for world peace. In 1994, I was back again at the invitation of Fabrice and Brigitte Corbin. They had learned about my earlier visit and invited me to see the bunker – they had restored it as a museum.

Fortunately, they had a great translator, Nicolas Dumont. We all became great friends.

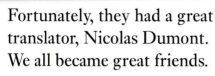

I even went back to the site of the first Bailey bridge we put across the Orne Canal just after D–Day.

From 1994, I returned to the bunker every year.

I got two more medals from the French Government.

Met my old mate, Piper Bill Millin...

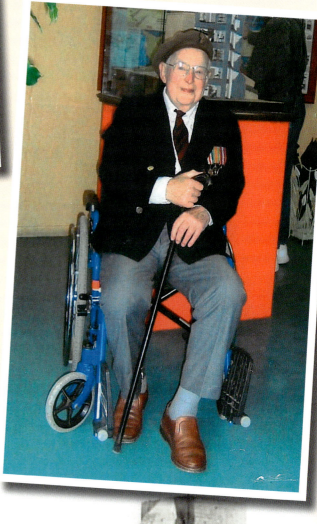

...and was always on hand at the bunker to answer questions, proudly being able to say, "I am the oldest thing in this museum" – which I was!

On my last visit, I took lots of school parties in to the bunker...

...and took my family over (well, most of them) for the 60th Anniversary of D-Day – my last visit.

14. FRANCE AND NEW ZEALAND

Our Maori-style welcome in New Zealand.

We loved the beautiful country.

I attend a peace conference in France,

lead the parade...

...and speak.

93

On our return from New Zealand, Nancy and I set up the "Environment and Peace Information Centre", or EPICENTRE, in Christchurch.

I still had some time to go walking with the family in one of my favourite places in the world, Cockley Beck in the Duddon Valley in the Lake District.

13. TO RUSSIA WITH PEACE

Our welcoming committee at the airport in Belarus, Russia.

Addressing the main peace conference in Moscow.

An evening with my son, Martin, and Professor Gregory Veikhman. Gregory had suffered terrible deprivation in Russia during the Second World War and was kept alive by our Arctic Convoys. He became an ardent peace campaigner and great friend.

This is the speech I gave in Moscow in 1991 – still so relevant today.

MOSCOW — JUNE 1991

50th ANNIVERSARY OF THE START OF THE
GREAT PATRIOTIC WAR OF THE SOVIET PEOPLE

Address by   Robert Orrell, Chairman,
British Ex-Services Campaign for Nuclear Disarmament.

I offer you all the Greetings and Good Wishes of the British Ex-Service Campaign for Nuclear Disarmament. We are a group of British War Veterans who have come together with the single purpose and objective to do all we can to prevent another World War, especially involving nuclear and other weapons of mass destruction.

I would like to add our thanks to our hosts for bringing us together on this occasion which commemorates a turning point in World History which brought many years of suffering to the Soviet Union and we can only hope that such an event will never happen again; I hope to devote my remaining years of life to this purpose.

At your gathering here over a year ago commemorating the end of that Great War of Liberation, I expressed the hope that one day, war veterans of the world who wish to see no more war, would unite together as one permanent organisation of Veterans from every country standing up together and saying with one voice, we will abolish war as a means of settling differences.

During the past year we have made a beginning towards such an organisation, and now have four nations in close and continuous contact under the name of the International Veterans for Peace Liaison Committee, with representatives from peace orientated Veterans Associations in France, U.S.A., Canada and Great Britain, and we welcome individuals or groups from other countries to join. I have further details for anyone who might be interested.

It began at the American Veterans for Peace Convention in August last year with the intention of keeping in close touch with one another and acting in unison in accordance with the principles of the Joint Statement of Veterans made here in Moscow in January 1988, should the need arise. The need did arise, sooner than expected and we acted in concert, all calling together on our governments on two occasions, first to avoid a conflict in the Gulf and then to make an early 'cease fire' after the slaughter had begun.

The War in the Gulf is a supreme example of a war that should never have happened; it has been of benefit to no-one except the manufacturers of armaments, brought tremendous and continuing suffering to vast numbers of innocent people and left the Middle East in a state of turmoil far worse than before. There is certainly no justification for victory celebrations, as are being held in London at the moment, and we are telling the people so today in a national newspaper.

When will we ever learn? Shall we never become civilised and find a way of controlling our aggressive instincts? It is absolute stupidity to accept war as a means of settling disputes. It saddens me that when parts of the world are moving towards Federation, as in Europe, at the same time other parts, and even within these European States, including Britain, are wanting to break away and establish their own separate tribal or religious groups which can only increase the probability of conflict between states.

We have a special place in the World today, we know what war is really like. We must not forget, we must tell the others and make them think; it is not just a T.V. game, it is the end of good in the World, of truth, of hope and of life itself. I do not need to say this to the Soviet People, who know it all so well, but we do forget, all of us. When shall we ever learn ?

Thank you for listening my friends. Try not to forget, and don't let your governments forget either.

Nancy and I believed passionately in a world free of nuclear weapons. She joined the Women's Peace Camp at Greenham Common, where US nuclear Cruise missiles were stationed.

She became involved in non-violent protest.

But when she made the gesture of "cutting the wire" at Greenham Common, she was fined. She would not pay the fine on a matter of principle and got two weeks in Holloway Women's Prison. We were all proud (but very worried for her too).

Me speaking at an Ex-Services CND peace conference in France. To my left, the great American peace hero George Mizo.

This is me in the 1990s. Nancy and I were now heavily involved in the peace movement – I even travelled to Vietnam on a peace mission.

I found demonstrating for a non-nuclear peace on the D–Day beaches quite scary. I still had my R.E.'s beret.

Just in case, I got a second sign done in French!

9. A WORLD WORTH FIGHTING FOR

Throughout the 1970s and 1980s I campaigned against war, particularly nuclear war. Firstly with Christchurch and New Forest CND, then in my capacity of Chairman of Ex-Services CND.

Nancy made me the military-style khaki suit, but I still proudly wore my R.E.'s beret and medals.

Nancy and I marching for peace – London in the early 1980s.

Marching through
London, then laying a
wreath at the Cenotaph...

...with other
ex-services people.

We were very well received and the
people, including the police, were
very friendly. There I am after
another 'ex-services' march and
Tony Benn is in the background.

We moved back to Christchurch when I retired. Our sons had always been keen Scouts: Nancy and I used to help make costumes for the gang shows. That became our business. The Costume Gallery meant I always had attire for any occasion.

As self-appointed town crier or...

...as Father Christmas, campaigning for World Peace

It also meant we saw more of Nancy's relations, particularly my brother-in-law, Ted, who was a great cartoonist. We built an extension to the gallery together (see next page).

6. REBUILDING MAIDSTONE

I landed the job of borough engineer and moved to the county town of Maidstone in Kent.

The front door of our house, Pickering Cottage. The impressive pillars each side of the door (holding up the porch roof) were rotting timber when wc moved in. The family rebuilt them using 8in drainpipes filled with concrete.

5. HOME SWEET HOME

Nancy and I were married in Christchurch Priory.

We spent time together, moving to a prefabricated home in Swindon shortly after the war. Here we are at peace in the hills.

My unit, 91st Field Company, was originally a beach group. We became a bridging unit a few weeks after D-Day and travelled all the way up to Holland, building bridges as we went, to keep our troops moving. This bridge over the Waal (lower Rhine) at Nijmegen, Holland, was built by our company. This photo shows us floating the last section in around August 1944.

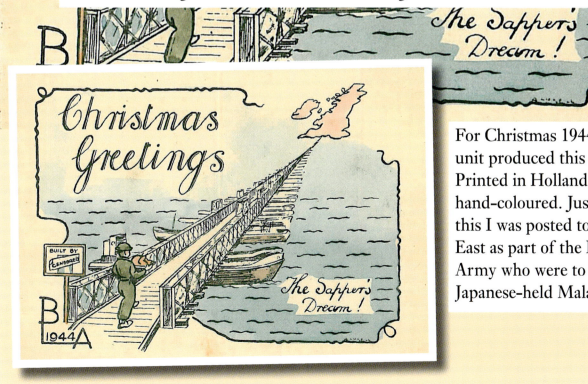

For Christmas 1944 our unit produced this card. Printed in Holland and all hand-coloured. Just after this I was posted to the Far East as part of the British Army who were to invade Japanese-held Malaya.

These are some of the Bailey Bridges that we built (and tested!) in Malaya.

Captain Walker, R.E. and me in
Bombay (now Mumbai) May 1945.

3. WE SAIL FOR FRANCE

It was a long crossing from embarking on Southsea beach, near Portsmouth. To me the sea seemed much rougher than this picture of the crossing shows. We were all very sick. The German shells falling all around might even have been a relief from the sea-sickness.

I landed about 4pm on D-Day. Much of the German resistance had been silenced by then. There was a great deal of debris on the beach, mainly our armour and beach obstacles, which our company set about clearing. I landed without getting my feet wet.

My colleagues of the British 3rd Infantry Division exiting Sword Beach at Ouistreham.

The position of 91 Field Coy. RE in the 'Order of Battle
Normandy Landing 6 June 1944

OPERATION OVERLORD
In Command of All Forces
(Eisenhower)
|
21st. Army Group
Land Forces Only
(Montgomery)
|
Brit. 2nd. Army
(Dempsey)
|
Brit 1st   Corps

JUNO BEACH   SWORD BEACH

Cdn. 3 Inf. Div Corps Troops   Brit 3rd Inf. Div.
101 Beach Sub-Area
6 Beach Group
91st. Field Coy. RE. ⊗
(%c Chris Harvey Maj. R.E)

Recce off (then ¾c) Lt. (then Capt) Bob Orrell R.E.

Mech Transport Sgt (also at Bunker) Jim Allmond R.E.

⊗ Before D-Day we trained with & were attached to 3 Brit. Inf. Div.
Shortly before the landing late reorganisation put us with 3 Cdn. Div
as they had decided not to use our 'Roger' beach section on the extreme
left. Soon we were back with 3 Brit. Div. & then later
directly under 30 Corps as we went through Europe into
Germany building Bailey Bridges over main rivers.
So - in some accounts 91 Fd Coy is
shown under 3 Cdn Div. and under   19. 3. 04
3rd Brit. Div in others. Both
are right.

My handwritten explanation of my own position in the order of battle on D-Day.

ARMY FORM C 2136 (Large)   MESSAGE FORM   Register No.

Call	Srl. No.	Priority	Transmission Instructions

ABOVE THIS LINE FOR SIGNALS USE ONLY.

FROM
(A) Recce Offr. 91 Field Company R.E   Date-Time of Origin. 14.00m 9/6/44

For Action.

TO   Commander Royal Eng'rs 6th. Beach Group

(W) For Information (INFO)

Officer Commanding 91 Field Coy R.E.

Office Date Stamp
Reply at 22.10 hrs gave order - "Investigate Bunker"

Message Instructions.

Originator's No.   R.O.3

Large supply of all types of engineering materials round German Strong Point, Map Ref 113 799. Todt Organisation constructing reinforced concrete gun positions before invasion. Stores on site :-
Concrete mixers 7/9 cuft. with chutes on staging ‑ ‑ ‑ 10
Cement in fair condition ‑ ‑ ‑ 50 tons
Steel bars 3/8" & 1/2" cut and bent ⟶, various 20 tons
Coils of barbed wire. 100 yd. rolls 20
Cut timber for shuttering approx 10 tons
Screwed steel tubing 2", 3" & 4"
Odd lengths of Rolled Steel Joists I; Gravel heap 50 tons
Large amount of electric cable, at least 2 generating sets
✗One large power house not yet investigated.
Building blocks 30 tn
Railway track & trucks, about 3/4 mile of track
Sundry tools, barrows etc.
Area very suitable for workshops & dump, but on sea shore presently in use as Anti Aircraft troop. No mines yet found, area not yet de-loused but our troops been here about 6 hours.
Exploder found connected to wires not yet traced. Sandy site suitable for making concrete.

This message may be sent AS WRITTEN by any means except WIRELESS. Signed. QDmll ✗	If liable to be intercepted or to fall into enemy hands this message must be sent IN CIPHER. Signed.	Originator's Instructions. Degree of Priority.	Time THI or TOR	System Cy.
			Time Cleared	

My report on 'Le Grand Bunker' three days after D-Day.

This shows the main Fire and Control Bunker in 1944, just after D-Day. Most of the houses had been cleared to give a clear field of fire and vision, all except two old buildings at the front, to partly conceal the bunker from the sea.

OUISTREHAM 1939-1944

Le PDT (« Grand Bunker ») après les combats. Photo prise par J. Lesage.

In the bombardment before D-Day a 'lucky shot' from HMS Frobisher hit the observation 'slit', putting the 'observation' bit of the bunker out of action.

The Bunker and Surroundings in 1944. An artist's impression, drawn from my memories, in 2002.

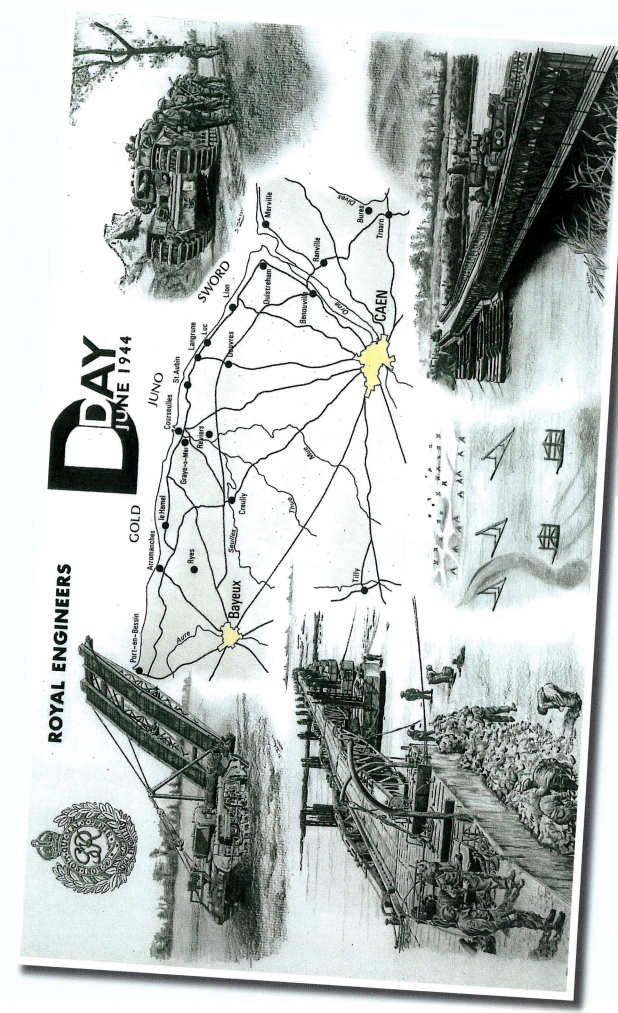

This nicely summarises the R.E.'s work during and after D-Day.

2. I JOIN THE ARMY AND FIND NANCY

My enlistment papers (after I volunteered for the Army), 29th May, 1940.

At Officer Cadet Training Unit (OCTU) in mid 1940.

Daily Express picture of officer cadets of the type being trained by Lieut.-Colonel (old school tie) Bingham, who has been ordered to explain to the War Office his letter saying that middle-class Army officers have "fallen down on the job."

From right to left are a civil engineer (grammar school), an engineer's assistant (grammar school); an assistant manager of a quarry (public school), a surveyor (secondary school), and an engineering student (technical school).

On an average only 8 per cent. of the cadets sent to this unit come from public schools. Ten per cent. are pre-war rankers, and the rest are either young men with university training (probably by their own efforts in scholarships) or men who left school at fourteen and went to evening classes.

It is seldom a man fails because of lack of leadership or military knowledge.

BRITISH SMASH INTO STREETS OF TOBRUK

▶ FROM PAGE ONE

their positions right up to the moment when the British troops burst through the barbed wire and cut them off from behind.

It is revealed now that the main British onslaught came down the macadam road leading in from Bardia along the coast. But it was launched simultaneously from all sections with the Free French taking a vital stretch of front line.

The Italians did not know from what direction the main weight of the British attack was going to come and when it did come we broke right through.

Many junior staff officers are among the captured.

"The whole operation has gone like Bardia," I was told at head-

fall of Koritza and Argyrocastro in Albania, Sidi Barrani in Egypt and Bardia in Libya.

Within our grasp tonight lies one of

Home on my first leave as 1st Lieutenant. I was still quite thin, for me, after my time in hospital.

When I was in OCTU, the Daily Express ran an article to prove that officers were not all from public schools. I'm the first in the rank, referred to as 'Civil Engineer' (Grammar School).

I make 2nd Lieutenant.

TRAINING FOR THE INVASION

Most of my time preparing for D-Day was spent in developing, testing and then training with 'THE BAILEY BRIDGE'... A fantastic invention.

As Montgomery writes later ... (in 1947) ...

"Bailey Bridging made an immense contribution towards final victory in World War II. As far as my own operations were concerned, with the Eighth Army in Italy and with the 21 Army Group in Northern Europe, I could never have maintained the speed and tempo of forward movement without large supplies of Bailey Bridging."

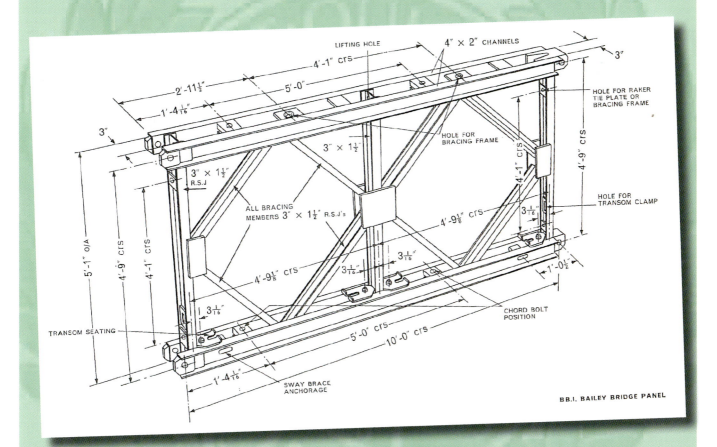

BB.I. BAILEY BRIDGE PANEL

The basic Bailey 'panel' could be carried by a team of six men; the panels formed both sides of the bridge, and could carry heavy loads over long spans, especially when 'doubled' or even 'tripled' up.

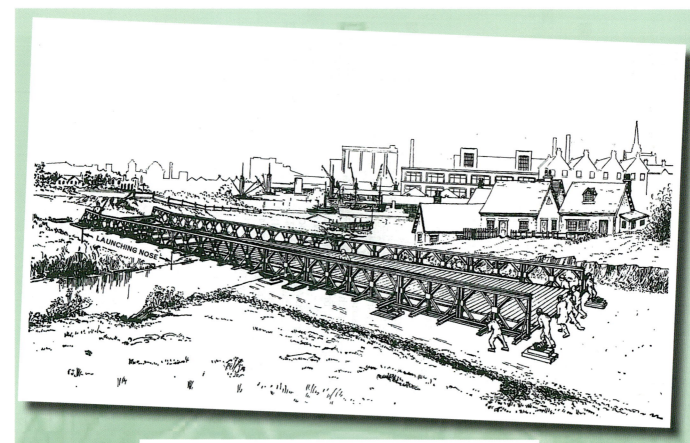

The Uniflote Handbook sketch of installing 'a Bailey'.

Testing an early 'Bailey Bridge' at Christchurch.

We also learnt about the GERMAN MINES we were likely to encounter: Anti-personnel mines such as the terrifying 'Jumping' S-mine (...the 'de-bollocker' as we later came to call it!).

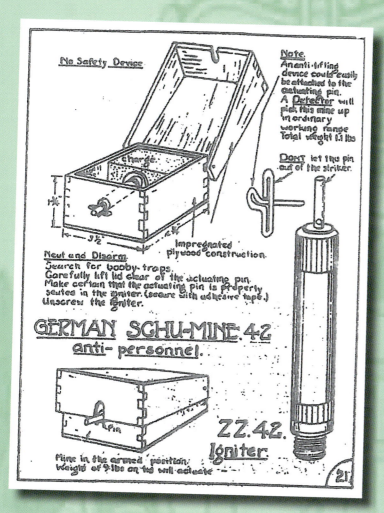

We were also expecting big and powerful 'Teler Mines'; not only buried, but also fitted to the beach obstacles we would have to clear.

Some mines came in wooden boxes (Schu-Mines), and the metal-free 'Pot Mines' were very difficult to find with our mine sweepers.

Everything we did was under the tightest security, as a cartoon in 'Punch' confirmed at the time...

Listen, Jane   *I've found out the date of—*   *you know what.*   *Unfortunately. I'm sworn to the most frightful secrecy—*   *so you'll just have to guess at it—*   *and I'll tell you when you guess wrong."*

MY EQUIPMENT FOR D-DAY

My main weapon was the MKII Sten Gun. It carried a magazine with a maximum of 32 x 9mm 'parabellum' rounds (the same ammunition as the German Schmeisser machine pistol – the idea was that we could then use captured ammunition).

By the time D-Day came, I was familiar with all the weapons used by the British Army. I had never fired a Sten Gun but that's what I was issued with.

The Mark II Sten Gun

I swapped my standard issue British bayonet for this great US 'Commando' knife. I kept this for the rest of my life. This is a photo of the actual knife; the blade is very slender now after repeated use and sharpening over 50 years!

As a reconnaissance officer, I was issued with the 'folding motorbike', which I used extensively in the first days after D-Day. Upon promotion to captain, shortly after landing, my 'happy wanderings' and days on the bike came to an end.

By the time I got to Malaya (now called Malaysia) I also carried a Gurkha 'Kukri' fighting knife, a marvellous tool for cutting your way through jungles. I brought this actual 'Kukri' back to the UK and used it in my garden all my life. My son now uses it in his garden!

Wherever I was, this photograph of Nancy was always with me.

1. EARLY YEARS

Me with my mother and father, Annie and Fred, in about 1922, aged four.

My Uncle Edgar (my father's brother) was killed in the First World War.

Aunt Rachel and I became close after my mother died in 1940.

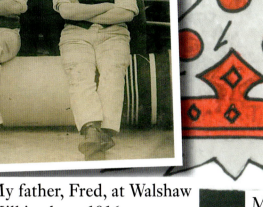

My father, Fred, at Walshaw Mill in about 1916.

My Aunt Joyce during the Second World War, a great support and family friend.

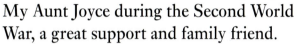

A charabanc to the seaside. My mother and father, Annie and Fred, (right in the front) about to set off for Rhyl, in Wales, for the day in 1910 or thereabouts.

Front/rear of the family home: 150 Booth Street, Tottington.

MY GRANDPARENTS

Mother Annie Warburton

My grandfather

Annie, Mary and Rachel.

Grandfather George   Grandmother

The Warburtons

And the Orrells

Bob's medals (these are the smaller 'dress' set). The full size ones are on display in 'Le Grand Bunker' - just inside the door which Bob 'blew'.

(Left to Right): The 1939–45 Star – The France and Germany Star with bronze oak leaf for Bob's 'Mention in Dispatches' for his Bunker Escapade – Defence Medal – War Medal 1939–1945.

By the KING'S Order the name of
Captain R. Orrell
Royal Engineers
was published in the London Gazette on
22 March, 1945,
as mentioned in a Despatch for distinguished service.
I am charged to record
His Majesty's high appreciation.

Secretary of State for War

Bob's letter from the King confirming his mention in despatches for taking 'Le Grand Bunker'.

By the same author:

Signalman Jones by Tim Parker
Brand: Seafarer Books

Shortlisted for the Maritime Media Awards 2011

Signalman Jones (later Lieutenant-Commander Geoffrey Holder-Jones DSM, VRD, RNVR) was born in Liverpool in 1915, and his remarkable exploits at sea during the Second World War are here told for the first time.

After he survived a German mine in the Thames estuary in 1939, the war took him, commissioned as a naval officer, to Iceland, Spitzbergen and the USA. Given command of his own ship, he patrolled the waters off Canada and Newfoundland before returning to Britain in 1944.

This true story, written by Tim Parker on the basis of personal conversations and a scrapbook entrusted to him 60 years after the war, illuminates one of the great mysteries of the war – the beating of the U-boat blockade of the American coast by squadrons that were little more than motley collections of armed trawlers and whalers.

A keen observer with an eye for the absurd, his story is short through with the good shipmate's sense of decency and humour that sustained him through the ordeals of convoy duty in the Arctic Ocean and the dark years of the war.

The Last Voyage of the Shelduck by Tim Parker
To be published in the Spring of 2014

The Last Voyage of the Shelduck is both a mystery and an affectionate portrait of an unusual group of people. It is a book that celebrates the English in its broadest sense.

The story is concerned with the repercussions of an incident that took place in the 1950's when Roxanne Goldberg, her friend Miles Sandford a formal Royal Navy Lieutenant and one Maurice Paul, a tailor, sailed in the Shelduck to Amsterdam to 'reclaim some important and valuable paintings from a private gallery in Amsterdam.

The novel opens some 50 years later. Roxanne Goldberg, now a redoubtable old lady, is living quietly in Brighton, taking regular holidays with her friends at 'The Sunshine', the second best hotel in Torquay. Then the past comes back to haunt, indeed to threaten her, her family and friends. While Alfred Askew, Mrs Goldberg's taxi driver finds himself with a Liebermann in his garden shed.

The book is illustrated throughout by David Diplock's remarkable drawings making the book a real treat.

LE GRAND BUNKER
MUR DE L'ATLANTIQUE
MUSÉE
OUISTREHAM
THIRD EDITION (APR

Our exciting, vivid and evocative displays (generator room, gas filters room, entrance protecting machine-gun emplacement, staff rest-room, first aid post, ammunition store, arms store, telephone operation room, radio transmission room and observation post with its range-finder which provides a panoramic view over the channel within a 25 miles radius) will help you to relieve history, the history of the people who had been waiting for the invasion for three years !

You will also be able to see many interesting and unpublished photos and documents about the atlantic wall, the biggest building site of the 20th century which employed over 2 million people.

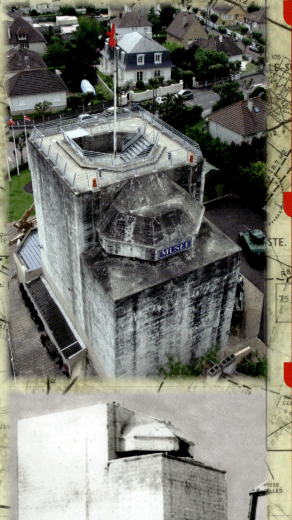

THE GRAND BUNKER AT OUISTREHAM A FANTASTIC SITE

Located at stones throw the beach and the ferry terminal, the Atlantic Wall Museum is inside the old german headquarter which was in charge of the batteries covering the entrance of the river Orne and the canal. The 52ft high concrete tower has been fully restored to make it look like how it was on the 6th of June 1944...

A POCKET OF GERMAN RESISTANCE

On six June, intrigued by this unforeseen obstacle, the Franco British commandos attempted to approach the Tower, but were repulsed by machine-gun fire and stick-grenades being thrown from the top. They were content to skirt the Bunker, which remained a permanent threat during the following days.

THE CAPTURE OF THE GRAND BUNKER

On 9 June, Lieutenant Bob ORRELL of Royal Engineers, 91 Field Company R.E., 3rd Beach Group, 3rd Canadian Div., 2nd British Army, was given orders to invest the large bunker. Accompanied by three men, he placed two explosive charges one after the other to blow up armour-placed door. Altogether it took them four hours to break it open ! The garnison of two officers and fifty men then surrendered the Liberation of Ouistreham was complete. The set of defensive works at Ouistreham shows the scate of construction work involved in the building of the Atlantic Wall.

Free parking nearby - Bookseller Specialized publications - Gift Shop
The museum is open from October 1 until March 31 : 10 AM to 6 PM
From April 1 until September 30 : 9 AM to 7 PM
Close January 9 until February 2

Avenue du 6 Juin - **14150 OUISTREHAM** - Calvados - FRANCE
Tél. : 02 31 97 28 69 / Fax : 02 31 96 66 05
www.musee-grand-bunker.com

Bob Orrell MICE

27th July 1918 – 30th June 2004

COU

M

GW01191296

TO FIND THE ANSWER WE MUST GO TO THE MAN AT THE HEART OF THE ORIGINAL EASTER STORY, JESUS CHRIST.

EVERY GENERATION has seen prophets, philosophers and politicians who have tried to change the world, only to fail, leaving it no better. Yet this man, Jesus, who was born in poverty, lived in obscurity, taught for no more than three years and left only a handful of followers behind him, truly transformed human civilisation.

When asked, 'What's wrong with the world?' by a newspaper, G.K. Chesterton responded, 'I am.'

So much of what we all value – the worth of every human regardless of their gender, power or wealth, the possibility of forgiveness, the importance of humility, the superiority of love for others – can be traced back to this Jesus. Indeed, for over two and a half billion human beings today, Jesus is not just the greatest of teachers but someone who is alive and can be known and worshipped as Saviour, Lord and God. At the heart of who Jesus was then and is today, lies Easter.

EASTER IS God's extraordinary answer to the problem that all humanity suffers from. Recognised in every age and culture, this is seen in the gulf between what we want to be and do and what we actually are and do.

THE BIBLE explains that this difference between the ideals and the reality of our lives is the working out of how, deep down, we are all separated from God. The Bible tells how, from the very beginning, we human beings have rebelled against the guidance of the one holy and loving God in order that we might live our own way.

THE RESULT of our stubborn independence can be seen in the pride, greed, selfishness, anger and hate that wreaks so much damage at every level, whether personal, national or global. We have all become separated from God, have all sinned and we all stand guilty. It's a bleak diagnosis, yet the Bible goes beyond it to speak of a God who in Jesus, and through Easter, brings hope.

'We live in a fallen world. There is a fundamental disorder in the universe which the Bible attributes to sin and alienation from God.'

John Stott

'From beginning
to end, the Holy
Scriptures testify
that the predicament
of fallen humanity
is so serious,
so grave,
so irremediable
from within,
that nothing short of
divine intervention
can rectify it.'

Fleming Rutledge

THE FIRST EASTER:
THE MAN

TWO THOUSAND years ago Jesus was born into a religious culture that recognised the separation between humankind and God.

THE OLD TESTAMENT records how, as a response to human rebellion, God sent his prophets who taught about him, priests who interceded before him and kings who ruled for him. These figures eased the problem of humanity but they couldn't bridge the chasm between humankind and God. God also sent promises and prophecies of someone 'who is to come', an individual who would stand between us and our maker. This figure – the *Messiah* – would be, at the same time, king and servant, priest and sacrifice.

IN THE NEW TESTAMENT, the four Gospels tell of how, in Jesus, the long-awaited Messiah finally arrived. They speak of what Jesus did and said, how he taught with wisdom, healed with power, gave orders to nature, liberated people from evil and, in his own authority, offered forgiveness.

'Take away the cross of Christ and the Bible is a dark book.'

J.C. Ryle

In words and actions Jesus showed to those prepared to listen that he was the ultimate and final prophet, priest and king. Indeed he went further, and by saying what only God could say and doing what only God could do, he claimed and demonstrated that he was more than a mere man. There is so much about Jesus that is unique.

JESUS' TEACHINGS are unique. What he taught was simple, authoritative and for everybody. Two thousand years of cultural change and technological advances have not eroded its value.

JESUS' CLAIMS are unique. He considered himself God's Son, took the titles for God as his own and spoke with God's authority. He claimed to be one with God; his followers believed him.

JESUS' ACTIONS are unique. He showed control over the natural and supernatural world, demonstrating his authority over people, things, spiritual powers and even death.

JESUS' CHARACTER is unique. Even the best human beings are flawed by weaknesses, inconsistencies and excesses. Yet in Jesus we see none of this. In him the virtues are balanced, complete and consistent. We see strength without harshness, gentleness without weakness, courage without rashness and authority without arrogance. With Jesus, forgiveness never became freedom of behaviour and friendship never slid into compromise. In Jesus we see the person we were meant to be and the person we wish we were.

'Jesus Christ is not
just "a" life,
but is "the" life.
He is not
just "a" truth,
but is "the" truth.
He is not
just "a" way,
but is "the" way.'

John Stott

THE FOUR ACCOUNTS of the life of Jesus in the New Testament of the Bible – Matthew, Mark, Luke and John – are ancient biographies. Where they can be checked with history they prove to be reliable.

At the psychological level they have the ring of truth. So at the first Easter we see a corrupt and worried religious leadership desperately agreeing to do wrong to save itself, and a governor of the occupying power panicking to avoid a career-ruining riot. There are evasions of responsibility, edgy power plays, uneasy moral compromises and a general atmosphere of chilling fear. Sadly, it's all true to life.

THE HISTORICAL authenticity of the Gospels is important. In the matter of how we live, die and spend eternity, what counts is fact, not fiction.

THE FIRST EASTER:
THE TRIAL AND TRAGEDY

FIRST, let me point out a striking fact: all four Gospels find Jesus' trial and execution incredibly significant. Every normal biography treats their subject's death as the end of their story. Yet the Gospels cover Jesus' crucifixion in such detail that it is perhaps the most well-described death in history. This emphasis on Jesus' death is common to all his first followers. Consider the following:

• From the earliest days Christians, following the command of Jesus himself, regularly met together to take bread and wine to be reminded of the broken body and the outpoured blood of his death.

- In many places in the Gospels, Jesus is reported as teaching that he must die and that his death would be deeply significant.

- Death by crucifixion was not just horrid and painful but also incredibly shameful. Indeed, Roman citizens were spared from it. Yet curiously, the early church didn't hide it as an embarrassing disgrace but proudly proclaimed it as a glorious triumph. In the letters of the early church the Christian message is sometimes just summarised as 'Jesus Christ and him crucified' **(1 Corinthians 2:2)**.

- Over the centuries by far the most common event from the New Testament depicted in art is the crucifixion. It's impossible to imagine any other figure of history being so frequently depicted suffering his or her death agonies.

LET ME SET THE STAGE for the events of the first Easter.

During the two or three years that Jesus taught, a growing confrontation between him and the religious leadership has grown. The leaders have a dominant and controlling religious system with a temple, sacrifices, priests and endless rituals and rules.

JESUS HAS, however, taught that none of this is needed for access to God. Indeed, he personally has offered forgiveness of sins. To make matters worse he has made increasingly open claims to be the long-awaited Messiah.

Matters have come to a head at a crowded celebration of the feast of Passover in Jerusalem, where the focus falls on God's dramatic liberation of his people some 1,500 years ago. The troubled and exasperated religious leadership decide that Jesus must be killed.

GIVEN THAT under Roman rule they lack the right to impose a death sentence themselves, they need to persuade the governor to do it for them. A Roman execution by crucifixion would have an advantage: its public and shameful death would confirm to all that Jesus was no real Messiah.

THE NEW TESTAMENT is clear, however, that it was not just human malice that caused the crucifixion. Jesus was no helpless victim dragged to a tragic end, but someone who chose to go to it. It's striking that at this first Easter, where everybody finds themselves outmanoeuvred by events, the one person who stays in control is Jesus – the victim. The New Testament is clear: behind the bitter hate and callous indifference of those hostile to Jesus lies the invisible but all-powerful hand of God.

'Jesus didn't come to earth for an **excursion** but an **execution**.'

anon.

FINALLY, JESUS is arrested at night and brought before the religious leaders. Under formal questioning he openly claims to be the Messiah, to be one with God, and the individual who will ultimately judge the world. So blasphemous are these claims that any hesitation over a death sentence vanishes.

Early in the morning of what has come to be called Good Friday, Jesus is hastily brought before Pontius Pilate, the Roman governor, and presented as a political threat to Rome. After interrogation, Pilate declares Jesus innocent and not deserving of death. Frustrated, the religious leadership persist in demands and threats until Pilate, fearful of a riot, yields and sentences Jesus to be flogged and crucified.

After a brutal flogging by mocking soldiers, a weakened Jesus carried the crossbar to the execution site where his arms were nailed to it. He was hoisted up on the vertical post and his feet were nailed to it. Then he was left to die.

ALMOST ALL methods of execution are designed to be swift and humane; crucifixion was, however, specifically intended to be the opposite: as painful and as long as possible. On a cross, the victim, often stripped naked, suffered shame, ridicule and agony for long hours and even days as, amid stench and screams, their bodies progressively failed and rotted.

Yet although crucifixion was appallingly cruel, the writers of the Gospels don't seek to either arouse our pity or our outrage. Rather, they speak of how what happened was a fulfilment or a completion of a mission. A most insightful phrase occurs in John's Gospel where in chapter 19 verse 30 we read that Jesus' final words were, 'It is finished.' The sense is not 'I am finished' but that 'my work is finished', 'my task is accomplished', even perhaps 'paid in full'.

THE GOSPELS tell how, in the afternoon, with his death brutally confirmed by the thrust of a Roman spear, Jesus' body was taken down. A burial party took him to a nearby grave site where he was hastily buried in an already excavated tomb, which was then sealed by a weighty stone. And that, according to every law of nature and history, should have been the end of the story of Jesus.

But it wasn't. Jesus, unique as ever, didn't stay dead.

THE FIRST EASTER:
THE TRIUMPH BEYOND THE TRAGEDY

ALL FOUR GOSPELS tell, in very different ways, how the tomb was found empty on the Sunday morning.

Then, in a series of varied occurrences over forty days, Jesus' followers met again with their Lord, now resurrected and alive beyond death.

THE ACCOUNTS say that the Jesus who they encountered was indeed the man who had been crucified and that he still bore the wounds inflicted on him. He had a physical body that could be touched and that allowed him to eat with his followers, yet at the same time he could appear, disappear and enter locked rooms. These appearances occurred to individuals and to groups, they happened outdoors and indoors, in daylight and at night. Notably, Jesus did not appear as some frail recuperating survivor from an appalling trauma but as someone full of power, authority and, above all, *life*.

THE EVIDENCE for the resurrection of Jesus remains remarkably strong. For a start it's not just the Gospels that speak of his resurrection but the

'The best news the world eve

entire early church. In Saint Paul's first letter to the Corinthians, chapter 15 is spent on the importance of the physical resurrection of Jesus. Indeed, all the letters of the New Testament refer to Jesus not as a figure of history but as a living, all-powerful being who is active in the world today.

There's the fact, too, that the universal confession of the early church was 'Jesus Christ is LORD', a statement that makes no sense unless he was indeed believed to be eternally alive and, in some way, God.

ad came from a graveyard.'

anon.

'One of the most astonishing aspects of the New Testament letters is how, when they refer to a man who had died, they use the present tense: Jesus **is**, not **was**.'

anon.

SUCH STATEMENTS were not just empty words. Many people in the early church went to their deaths and even torture and execution, confident that Jesus had triumphed over death. The message swept across the Mediterranean within a few decades, and the known world within a few centuries.

If Jesus had not risen, he and his followers would have been at most a tiny footnote in a multi-volume encyclopaedia of Middle East religions.

THE FACT remains that throughout Christian history, believers have been able to testify to a personal conviction that in, and through, Jesus they have come to know and love God.

'Perhaps the strongest statement we can make about the resurrection . . . is that if Jesus had not been raised from the dead, we would never have heard of him.'

Fleming Rutledge

THE FIRST EASTER:
THE REASON WHY

THE NEW TESTAMENT consistently teaches that the cross was not a brutal accident but an achievement.

Indeed, the resurrection is seen primarily as a powerful confirmation that Jesus was all he claimed to be and that the task he had undertaken on the cross was a success. With the resurrection Jesus goes from being *victim* to *victor*; the one who has triumphed over evil, sin and death.

IF WE READ THE GOSPELS, and indeed the whole New Testament, the intense focus on the cross raises the sharpest of questions: what was the point of Jesus' death there?

Let me suggest four things.

1) AT THE CROSS GOD REVEALS WHO WE ARE

At the first Easter we see the most tragic of stories. We watch a man who is innocent, loving, truthful, having a godly authority and who fulfils all that his faith has looked forward to. He arrives at its religious centre at the time of its chief ceremony and instead of acceptance and acclaim he is rejected, mistreated and brutally executed.

THE CROSS reveals the gap between humanity and God with a terrible clarity. There is, too, no single villain.

True, the religious leadership cynically agree to sacrifice the one who should be their king. But the political leadership

'Jesus has forced open a door that had been locked since the death of the first man. He has met, fought and beaten the King of Death. Everything is different because he has done so.'

C.S. Lewis

rejects what is right and, out of fear, has an innocent man die horribly. The disciples fail miserably: Judas betrays Jesus, Peter denies knowing Jesus and the other disciples flee in fear.

The crowd, having shifted allegiance, savagely demands blood. The soldiers obey orders and perform their task with unthinking brutality; the spectators gawp and jest at the dying man. It's not a pretty sight.

AND LET'S NOT PASS THE BLAME onto some other people separated from us by time, culture or race. In our own way, we all commit similar sins of a lesser nature.

The story of the first Easter is like some vast, busy painting full of interacting characters centred around the figure of Jesus, and if you look carefully and honestly at it you can have the unnerving experience of glimpsing yourself in the shadows. Each of us stands before God as those who are accused, are guilty and await judgement.

THE CROSS is a good visual image. Angled as an **X**, it is the sign of a wrong answer and it is a *condemnation*. It says over every human life – yours and mine – that we have got it utterly wrong.

2) AT THE CROSS GOD REVEALS WHO HE IS

If the cross of Christ tells us how bad we are, it also tells us how good God is. Many people see God as some permanently angry and accusing being who is only waiting to pour out judgement on us worthless men and women.

Yet the cross says otherwise. Consider the following Bible verses:

- 'For God so loved the world that he gave his one and only Son, that whoever believes in him shall not perish but have eternal life.' **(John 3:16)**

- 'I have been crucified with Christ and I no longer live, but Christ lives in me. The life I now live in the body, I live by faith in the Son of God, who loved me and gave himself for me.' **(Galatians 2:20)**

- 'Live a life of love, just as Christ loved us and gave himself up for us as a fragrant offering and sacrifice to God.' **(Ephesians 5:2)**

IN FACT, the New Testament says that in the cross we see God's love for us magnificently and clearly revealed. Here he treats us as having supreme value and he cares for us with a deep love. The truth of the cross is that God is indeed a judge but that, out of his love for us, he lets the judgement fall on himself!

Let's return to that visual image. Angled again as a neat **X** we see the cross as a sign of *devotion* in love and loyalty. It says how much we are worth to God.

WHEN ON 15th April 2019 fire broke out in the roof of the great medieval cathedral of Paris' Notre Dame and rapidly spread, it was soon obvious that there was the likelihood that the

'What brought
Jesus to the cross
was ultimately
not the authorities
of the Jews and
the Romans
but God's love
and purpose.'

anon.

whole structure, at the centre of a nation and its history, would collapse. Despite not knowing if they would ever come back out, hundreds of fire fighters entered the blazing building to save it. They were prepared to sacrifice their lives for something of enormous value.

In the horror of the cross, God makes a statement of how much he loves and values us.

3) AT THE CROSS GOD RESCUES US FROM WHO WE ARE

The New Testament sees the cross as a triumph. The very word *gospel* means 'good news' and it is indeed the very best news of all.

THE BIBLE explains that in some awesome, ultimately incomprehensible way, Jesus' death was where God took on *himself* the penalty that should have been ours and paid for it. As Paul says in **Romans 5:8**, 'But God demonstrates his own love for us in this: while we were still sinners, Christ died for us.'

The first Easter occurred at Passover when sacrifices were offered, and the New Testament claims that, on the cross, Jesus became the ultimate sacrificial animal. He was 'the Lamb of God, who takes away the sin of the world' **(John 1:29)**.

Understanding – as far as is possible – how this worked is helped by the claim that Jesus was both perfect man and perfect God. By representing both sides, he could be a mediator. As a human being he had the right to stand in our place, and as eternal and infinite God he had the power to save us.

At the first Easter, Jesus substitutes for us: the innocent changing places with the guilty so that we who are guilty might be declared innocent. Behind the cruelty of the cross lies the deepest, richest and most sacrificial love.

ONE HELPFUL way of thinking about this is to recognise that, in many cultures, a family is seen so united together that one member can stand in for another.

So when, at a time of war, there is conscription and a son is called up for military service, his brother may be accepted in his place. Given that to become a Christian is to become part of the family of God, it's a helpful thought that when it comes to judgement, Jesus, our elder brother takes our place.

At the cross a loving God offers us a costly rescue, and pays the price himself!

LET'S RETURN to the cross as a visual image. Angled as an **X** and written large and bold, it can be the sign of a *cancellation*. A bill or a charge sheet against us is, in a significant phrase, 'crossed off'.

Paul writes in **Colossians 2:13-14** that God 'forgave us all our sins, having cancelled the charge of our legal indebtedness, which stood against us and condemned us; he has taken it away, nailing it to the cross'.

4) AT THE CROSS GOD RESTORES US TO WHO WE WERE MEANT TO BE

So the cross offers forgiveness to those who want to receive it.

But the cross doesn't just offer a formal legal verdict of 'declared innocent' or 'case dismissed'; it goes further. It offers a new, richer and fuller life. God offers us restoration and reconciliation.

WITH THE PRICE of our rebellion paid and the record against us cancelled, we can now know God not as judge, but as a loving, perfect father – the ideal parent – and we can have Jesus as our loving older brother. God is now the one who cares for us and who stands alongside us in life and in death.

'The resurrection is the proof of our reconciliation.'

Geoffrey B. Wilson

THERE'S A GOOD ILLUSTRATION of the way the cross changes lives at the heart of *Les Misérables*, whether in the book, on screen or stage. The desperate and hardened criminal Jean Valjean steals a bishop's silver but is caught. The bishop not only forgives him but gives him some valuable silver candlesticks as well. The rest of the story tells how Jean Valjean, shaken by this extraordinary and shocking act of grace, responds by seeking to live a good life.

THE BELIEVER in Christ is aided in living a new and better life by the Holy Spirit. Forty days after his resurrection, Jesus ascended to that dimension beyond our world that we call 'heaven'. From there God has sent himself into the world as the Holy Spirit, as a gift to all believers in Jesus so that they can have the same relationship to God as the disciples had with Jesus on earth.

THE HOLY SPIRIT is also an agent of transformation, helping us show God's characteristics of love, joy, peace, patience, kindness, goodness, faithfulness, gentleness and self-control – what the Bible calls the fruit of the Holy Spirit **(Galatians 5:22-23)**.

LET'S RETURN to that visual image a last time. Returned to its vertical form and written as ✚ the cross represents an *addition*; the positive adding on of something. The cross is not just a cancellation of the bad news of our debt before God, it adds good things to our lives. We have a new relationship with God and are given the power of the Holy Spirit.

One aspect of the achievement of Easter is vital – it throws a dazzling light into that harsh element of existence that haunts all life: *death*.

AS CHRIST undertook to suffer death for all who trust in him, believers in him can trust that as he rose from death, so they will one day rise. One of the great preachers of the past captured the meaning of the resurrection in a sermon sharply titled 'The Death of Death in the Death of Christ'.

CONCLUSION

To commit yourself to the living Christ of Easter is to trust in the cross and the resurrection and to move into a transformed situation.

YOU ARE FORGIVEN, God is now your friend and Jesus is your older brother. You have the possibility of a new existence that is aided and empowered by God's own Holy Spirit. Easter is the truth on which you can build a life or rebuild a damaged one.

BY NEAR universal agreement, William Shakespeare is held to be the greatest writer of plays. In Stratford-upon-Avon where he was buried in 1616, there is a statue overlooking Shakespeare's grave that depicts the great man in the process of writing with a quill pen, the original of which has long since vanished. It is, however, replaced every year on the anniversary of his death, when the old and weathered quill is slid out and a new quill slipped in.

'Without Christ
we have a
hopeless end,
but with Christ
we have an
endless hope.'

anon.

It's a touching ceremony but it reminds us that the long-dead Shakespeare has stopped his life's work of writing. In stark contrast, Easter speaks of a Jesus who is still alive and indeed is still at work in the world.

I have given Jesus permission to write my life; will you let him write yours?

IF YOU want to accept the truth of Easter, let me offer you this prayer.

Dear Jesus,

Thank you for dying on the cross for me. I know I have done many things wrong in thought, word and deed, and I ask you to forgive me. Cleanse and heal my life and set me free from the past. I invite you into my life now – come in by your Holy Spirit. Fill me with your presence, peace and power. Help me from this day on to follow you.

Amen.

If you want to know more about Jesus, the meaning of the cross and the reality of the resurrection, I recommend the book I wrote with Chris Walley: *Jesus Christ – The Truth*.

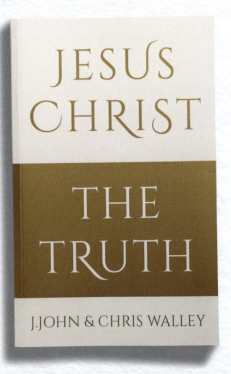